# ROWING

# ROWING

Silken Laumann with Calvin Wharton

Photography by Michael Cullen • History by Peter King

(Stoddart)  A BOSTON MILLS PRESS BOOK

**Canadian Cataloguing in Publication Data**
Laumann, Silken, 1964-
     Rowing

Includes bibliographical references.
ISBN 1-55046-083-8

1. Rowing - Canada. 2. Rowing - Canada - History.
I. Wharton, Calvin, 1952-     . II. King, Peter. III. Title.

GV797.C2L3  1994          797.1'23'0971     C94-930286-4

First published in 1994 by
Stoddart Publishing Co. Limited
34 Lesmill Road
Toronto, Canada
M3B 2T6
(416) 445-3333

A BOSTON MILLS PRESS BOOK
The Boston Mills Press
132 Main Street
Erin, Ontario
N0B 1T0

Design by Gillian Stead
Printed in Singapore

The publisher gratefully acknowledges the support of the Canada Council,
Ontario Ministry of Culture and Communications, Ontario Arts Council,
and Ontario Publishing Centre in the development of writing and
publishing in Canada.

# ACKNOWLEDGMENTS

In researching and preparing this text, I wish to thank the following people for permission to refer to their work: Chris Flood, for his book on the history of sport in Saint John; Stephanie Brooks, for her master's thesis on Jake Gaudaur; Paul Beedling, for his thesis on Joe Wright Jr. and Jack Guest; and Jack Carver, for his book on the history of the Vancouver Rowing Club.

Peter King

Completing this book required quite a bit of travel across Canada. Along the way I was helped by a great many people—coaches who took me in their boats, athletes who allowed me to disrupt their workouts, and many friends who let me sleep in an extra bed. There are several people whom I would like to thank personally. First, there is my brother, Munro Cullen, and my close friend Michael Montague, who acted as my assistants on trips, helping with the driving, carrying cameras and sometimes running the motorboats. Sandra Hudson and Bob Maguire in Victoria, Rob Marland and Jane Forsyth in Ottawa, Price Montague in Vancouver, Mernie and Rodney James in Okatoks, Alberta, Jamie and Laurie Chapman in Toronto, the Sawler family in Halifax, and Mark Lowery in Ottawa, all made important contributions of time and effort. I would like to thank national team coaches Mike Spracklen and Allan Morrow for giving me access to their athletes, and the national team athletes themselves, for letting me witness the realization of their dreams.

I'm grateful to John Denison from Boston Mills Press for having the idea for this book in the first place and for having the good sense to invite me to participate. Gill Stead, who designed this book, has done a wonderful job of editing ten thousand photographs into a coherent form. Nikon Canada should also be thanked, for lending me equipment for extended periods and not complaining when the equipment was returned with watermarks.

Finally, I would like to thank my wife, Lisbeth Shaw-Cullen, and my two children, Grace and Sean. Without their support and understanding this project would never have been completed.

Michael Cullen

# CONTENTS

PREFACE                                   7

A SPORT FOR EVERYONE                     11

TRAINING                                 23

COACHING                                 33

SINGLE SCULLING                          45

TEAMWORK                                 59

CLUB ROWING                              71

RACE DAY                                 83

NATIONAL TEAM ROWING                     95

HISTORY                                 109

   Introduction                        109

   Early History                       109

   The Maritimes                       111

   The Rise of the Amateurs            123

   After the Second World War          132

   The Change                          136

   World Medals Won by Canadians       143

ENDNOTES                                151

BIBLIOGRAPHY                            152

*Ottawa Rowing Club scullers row out into the Ottawa River.*

*Silken Laumann on Elk Lake.*

# PREFACE

As Calvin Wharton and I talked to more and more rowers about rowing—what it meant to them, why they enjoyed it—commonalities began to emerge. They told stories about the thrill of competition, the friendships they had developed, the beauty of a boat moving through water. Rowers talked to us about their greatest races, the thrill of winning, the fun of rowing as a team. They effused about their favourite coach, their best teammate, and their highest moment in the sport—there is nothing moderate about the way rowers feel about rowing. But the thing they talked about most passionately was what rowing had taught them.

Rowing is a great teacher. When the medals are old and dusty, my real memories will be of how I found a pureness on a river in a wooden boat, the pureness of a pursuit whose greatest reward is the knowledge that you have tried, and tried with all your might. The strokes down the river teach me. They show me how hard life can be, how long it can take to get what you want, and ironically, how getting what you want is often the least important part of the experience.

Rowing is not only what I do, it is a big part of who I am. Many rowers share the same conviction. In a few years the starting line of an Olympic final will cease to be a driving force in my life and career, and family will be top priority. But the sport will not leave me, for it has shaped me and it is there in all the decisions I make. The honesty I look for in business relationships is the honesty I have come to expect from coaches and teammates. There is nowhere to hide in the sport of rowing. A hard work-out demands that you be honest about effort and commitment and who you really are. On a starting line, appear-ances, social status, and all that stuff that divides people don't exist. It is this simplicity and clarity that people seek and find in rowing, and it is a clarity that rowing leads me to look for in other parts of my life.

Rowing is undergoing a lot of changes. Canadian rowing clubs are bursting at the seams as more and more people become interested in the sport. The tremendous success of the Canadian women's and men's Olympic teams in Barcelona brought rowing into living rooms across the country. Many young people now see rowing as something they would like to try. Parents are enrolling their kids in summer learn-to-row programs, while high-school rowing attracts thousands of new people each year. I believe the new-found popularity of rowing will help bring it to smaller communities, communities that until now have not been able to sustain a rowing club. Increased enrolment will put a strain on existing clubs, but with time and a few growing pains these clubs will adapt and enjoy the energy that the new converts bring to the sport.

Each time we welcome an athlete to the sport, we gain a friend, and we share with her or him something that has enriched our lives. It is a thrill to watch people of all ages and levels of ability find similar joy in the sport. When eighty-one-year-old Ken Clarke talks to me about the exhilaration he feels today because of his per-fect row—"The boat was just gliding across the water"—I feel a connection to him, because I have felt the same exhilaration. When a rower has gained enough skill to make the boat glide through water, he or she wants to share this feeling with others. There is a tremendous tra-dition of giving back to rowing. Most athletes want to

*Start of the Men's Lightweight Eight at the Ontario Championships on the Welland Canal.*

*Quidi Vidi Lake, St. John's, Newfoundland*

give back what they have learned, by coaching, by being club board members, by staying involved with the sport.

Each chapter of this book highlights a different aspect of Canadian rowing. Chapters on training, coaching, teamwork, competition, and national team and club rowing share with the reader experiences that rowers, parents of rowers, and officials and coaches have had with the sport.

Rowing is largely a team sport, and in writing this book we had our own team. Michael Cullen, Calvin Wharton, Peter King and I all worked with Boston Mills Press managing editor Noel Hudson to make a whole.

Michael Cullen's knowledge of and love for rowing speak to us from his photographs. He captures the joy, the exaltation, and the peace of rowing. He takes us into some of the sport's magic moments, otherwise only experienced by putting a boat on the water. Michael Cullen's photographs are a celebration of Canadian rowing.

Calvin Wharton was introduced to rowing by working with me during the writing of this book. Many hours spent speaking to rowers piqued his curiosity about the sport, and a few months ago he tried it for himself. Perhaps amidst all the talk about the tranquillity of rowing I forgot to remind Calvin how tippy a rowing shell can be. It is reassuring to know that even a sudden dunk in cold water and the loss of a pair of eyeglasses didn't dampen his enthusiasm for the sport. Without Calvin's assistance, writing this book would have been impossible.

Finally, Peter King gives us an important historical perspective on Canadian rowing; he reminds us of the proud history we have in this sport.

Then and now, we have a lot to celebrate.

9

*Members of the Lake Louise (Alberta) Rowing Club work out.*

# A Sport for Everyone

*The other people in the boat don't want to know what your background is. They don't care if you're a lawyer or a labourer. The common denominator is rowing, and your friendship is based on skill and enthusiasm for the sport.*
—Marilyn Copland, a director of the Victoria Rowing Club and a masters rower

For most people, the word "sport" has vivid connotations. In North America, it usually brings to mind the image of professional competitions involving highly paid (generally male) athletes who range in age from about twenty to forty and are almost always at the peak of physical condition. This vision makes more people fans than participants.

Rowing, however, is a sport that's accessible to almost everybody, and one that has its roots firmly planted many hundreds of years ago in the history of humankind. Today, in Canada, people of all ages enjoy rowing. In fact, it's one of the few sports you can successfully pick up in your later years without ever having tried it in your youth. It's also an activity that provides the excitement of competition or can be savoured purely for its recreational value, or both. Recently, young and old have taken to this sport in unprecedented numbers. According to Rowing Canada Aviron, the sport's national governing body, there were about seven thousand registered rowers in 1993. And although the organization points out that these numbers don't reflect all rowers, just those they can count, the figure is almost double that of a year earlier.

Bruce Trewin, captain of the Vancouver Rowing Club, feels that the high profile of Canadian rowers following the 1992 Olympics is largely responsible for this growth. "After Barcelona, the media brought the public's attention to rowing," he explains. "Following wins in '84 [in Los Angeles] there was a surge of interest, but nothing like this time, because now the media have caught on."

Rowing is one of the most aesthetically appealing sports. You're outside, often at sunrise or sunset; everything seems so peaceful; and when the boat is going well, it literally cuts through the water. Even the boats, or shells, have an aesthetic appeal—they are beautiful, handmade objects that reflect the many hours of careful labour that go into their construction.

Two basic forms make up the sport of rowing: sculling, in which rowers each hold two oars; and sweep, in which they hold only one oar apiece. Within these two categories are a number of different boats accommodating one, two, four or eight rowers. Some boats include a coxswain, who steers by controlling the rudder with foot pedals, and who directs the rowers. The length of the boats ranges from around 8 metres for a single, to about 17 metres for an eight. Despite their length, the shells are remarkably lightweight—my racing scull is light enough, at 15 kilograms, that I can carry it quite comfortably over my head to the water.

But aside from all the media attention rowing has drawn lately, why are so many people becoming involved in it? Perhaps because, as Sam Craig, founder of Toronto's

*The rowing display at the Maritime Museum of the Atlantic in Halifax, Nova Scotia.*

*The Canadian women's quad following their gold medal performance at the Universiade.*

Hanlan Boat Club and former president of Rowing Canada, says, "Rowing's not likely to hurt you, and you're going to get a lot out of it. Because of the amount of time involved in the sport, most rowers can't do a lot of other things. But nobody's got a gun to my head; I do it because I want to." Or maybe because it's largely a participative sport, as Moe Cody, secretary of the Nova Scotia Rowing Association says. "If you're only a spectator," he claims, "rowing can be considered dull. You can't see the whole of a race unless you're alongside in a boat."

Or possibly, the sport is simply addictive, as Bruce Trewin claims: "You get really hooked on it. Rowing is unlike other sports. It's almost never your team against another team—it's not a winner/loser thing, but a series of winners at different levels. At a regatta, you may win some and lose some, but there's a very positive mentality, almost never any bitterness. It's a kind of fraternal mixing. Also, the feeling of being out in the boat, just you and the water,

no motor involved—it's hard to describe this to anyone. Racing is almost incidental for most people; they enjoy the training."

In addition, rowing is relatively easy to learn, so beginners are soon able to get out on the water and enjoy themselves. But it takes a long time to learn to row well. It's a highly technical sport; you have to think about every movement, and at the same time not think about them. In the end it has to come naturally, almost as if there's no thought involved. Good rowing appears effortless, yet takes a lot of work to achieve.

"Rowing requires total concentration," says Trewin. "You have to be aware of what's going on. During the two-second duration of a stroke, there are many things that have to be done right. You experience moments of perfection, then they're gone."

Part of the reason for the rising numbers is the inclusion of women in the sport. Although relatively uncom-

*Rowing inside the breakwater at the Argonaut Rowing Club, Toronto.*

mon, women have participated in rowing for decades. But not until 1974 did women compete internationally. That year's world championships, the first to be designated "world," was also the first appearance of women rowers at international regattas, and the 1976 Olympics in Montréal marked the first time women rowed in the games. "The sport has exploded here since," says Claude Saunders, a former Olympic oarsman, and chair of the Royal Canadian Henley. "It's at the point where, in the '93 Henley, sixty percent of the competitors were women. Look at their

amazing performance in the last Olympics. They're a power in the sport and have given a tremendous boost to rowing."

Not only do rowing participants cross the gender barrier, they also range in age from teens to octogenarians. Kenneth Clarke is a Victoria rower who began rowing in Winnipeg in 1931. Clarke says he only rowed for about five years, then stopped until 1992, when he returned to the sport at the age of eighty. "I had no time for rowing," he says, "and I've regretted that many times. When I quit, I

*McGill crew and unofficial mascot at the 1993 Eastern Ontario Rowing Championships.*

never intended to take it up again, but we had a place on the lake, and every time I saw a glassy surface on the water, I thought, Wouldn't it be nice to be out on that in a shell?" A while ago, Clarke saw a shell on display in a shopping mall, so he went down to the Victoria City Rowing Club to see if he could get out on the water. Now he rows every few days. "I had some tests," he says, "and they discovered a little heart murmur. But the doctor said, 'Go ahead; just remember you're eighty.'"

I've watched Clarke row on Elk Lake and can testify that the tall, slim senior is adept in a single scull. He's technically still a very good rower. "People are always surprised that I'm rowing at my age," he says. "Well, I'm just as surprised. I've lost about fifteen pounds and feel in fine shape. I'm amazed the rowing doesn't tire me at all. I've never felt old, but the mere fact I'm fascinated with rowing and want to achieve racing ability—I suppose that's feeling younger. Now I want to try my hand rowing against others in my age group."

On the other end of the age spectrum are the high-school kids who take up rowing. Young rowers are essential to the development of the sport in Canada. They provide a basis for our future national teams. As Claude Saunders says, "We build rowing from the club level up. It's important to bring out the high-school kids, because

*National team member Derek Porter training at Elk Lake, British Columbia.*

out of a hundred who begin, only ten will stay in the sport. If kids fall in love with rowing in high school, they'll stay with it the rest of their lives."

One of these is Annelise Hall, a seventeen-year-old rower from Delta, British Columbia, who began in the sport in the summer of 1992. "My friend and I couldn't do many sports because of our body shape," she explains. "So we thought we'd try rowing and joined the high-school team. My dad's now on the executive of the Delta Deas club; we joined at the same time. My mom and sister don't understand rowing, and a lot of my friends think it's a wimpy sport, but I say it's the most demanding sport there is. Rowing's not only a physical challenge, but a mental challenge, too. By the time I'm three-quarters through a race, I feel finished. But my partner and competitors keep me going."

Rowing is a wonderful sport for girls and women who are perhaps a bit awkward, tall, and/or who feel kind of big (which more or less describes me when I began rowing). You can be heavy and still do it well. Some of the kids who become involved don't have the same self-esteem as those drawn to other sports. Unlike basketball, for example, where competition to make the team is tough, a lot of kids try out for rowing initially because nobody gets cut from the rowing team.

*There was no high-school rowing when I was a kid—that's what they called me, "Kid." Now they call me "The Boss."*
—Theo Dubois, 82-year-old Winnipeg rower

*Senior oarsmen carry their boat into the boathouse at the Argonaut Rowing Club, Toronto.*

*Putting the oars back on the rack at the Thunder Bay (Fort Williams) Rowing Club.*

Among rowers, age barriers are uncommon. Whether they're seventeen or seventy, rowers can generally communicate, since they share a love of rowing. There's also very little ego involved in the sport. In part, that's because there's little money, few TV cameras and almost no public focus on rowing. As well, there's a lack of tolerance for ego; if individuals or groups become arrogant, someone will quickly point this out to them. This tends to keep relationships within the sport quite simple. The media may occasionally treat you as if you're something special, but around other rowers you're no different than the person rowing next to you.

Lorne Loomer is a Victoria rower who won a gold medal at the 1956 Olympics as part of Canada's four. This crew is sometimes referred to as the "golden four" because their win surprised everyone. Even now, the soft-spoken Loomer takes very little credit for the achievement, placing most of the merit on his teammates and especially his coach, Frank Read. "I've heard it said that a coach is probably ten or twenty percent of a crew," Loomer says. "But I really feel that, for us, Frank was ninety-five percent. We were only the medium through which he was acting."

Loomer also feels that rowers are unique individuals: "I would like to think that I could pick the rower from among a group of people. Not only because they're generally a foot and a half taller than everyone else, but because they act like men and women who have lost their ego through rowing. By giving that up, they've gained something. Rowing is meant for special people—not special big or strong, necessarily, but people who like a challenge and aren't afraid of a commitment."

Loomer himself is one of these types, although I doubt he would ever claim to be. In 1990 he suffered a stroke and wound up in the hospital. "At the time, it seemed so impossible that I would ever talk or even walk again," he says. "An old friend and fellow rower, David Anderson, visited me regularly. I was swimming and working with a physiotherapist, and wasn't even anticipating getting back into a shell, because the therapists had said that rowing wouldn't be beneficial for me. But David talked me into it. Now it's been over a year since I've been going out there. Everyone's been quite good to me. I can't get in and out so slickly anymore, but that's the wonderful thing about rowing, that they would welcome me. Rowing's been great for my recovery. The physical part is only a portion of it; there's also the mental part, to be accepted by people. I love it when they tease me." Loomer now rows several times a week in a modified coxed double, with the coxswain's seat removed to accommodate a third rower.

In some ways, I can relate to Loomer's experience of recovery through rowing. In 1992, after a German rower in Essen collided with me and tore the muscle away from my leg, I felt that I was tested. I don't think I became a different person that summer, or that anything significant in my character changed. I feel it's easy to be optimistic, hardworking and dedicated when you're not faced with major difficulties. However, that was such an obvious obstacle for me. What I've learned in my years of rowing is how to face challenges. Each time I'm faced with a new one, I remember that I got through all the previous ones, and that gives me a certain perspective on life.

I've also learned how to separate priorities and set goals. Since I was young, I've had a sense of urgency, that life and time are short. This is not in a crazy sense, but more, How can I do all the things I want to accomplish? Until the day I die, I'll write down what I need to do each day, and set goals for every year. Being involved in rowing has taught me this.

Of course, rowing is not only useful in terms of rehabilitation and self-discipline, as Frank Read points out: "Rowing is such wonderful exercise. It puts your body in beautiful shape; it's one of the healthier sports. If you're introduced to it properly, and do it properly, you should never have any injuries from rowing. It uses all the mus-

*Pennsylvania Athletic Club crew, with coxswain in the bow of the boat, at the Royal Canadian Henley Regatta.*

*Mexican oarsmen stay out of the sun at the Royal Canadian Henley.*

*Carol Love (far right), Women's Eight bronze winner at the 1977 World Championships, 1976 Olympian, and coach, watches the start of a race at the Head of the Trent Regatta with four of her five children.*

cles, and you can work as strenuously or as gently and smoothly as you like. They used to say it was hard on the heart; now they talk about the longevity of the oarsperson."

Mel Laforme is a rower who competed on the national team quadruple crew in four Olympics, from 1976 to '88. "I've been active in a variety of sports," he says, "but after being involved in rowing—not only in training, but in many other aspects—and considering what it's about and what's required of you, other sports are sort of pretend; something seems missing.

"Rowing is always a break for me. It's a recharge, invigorating in a psychological way. I work as a teacher and I still row. Many of the people I work with don't have the same kind of outlet. When they look at me, they have trouble understanding how I deal with things, or why my perspective is the same in June as in September. I'm not saying I'm better at it, but that rowing gives me that ability."

The rewards of the sport are tangible, but the self-discipline and commitment translate into a lot of early mornings and hard work. Especially on a competitive level, rowing requires dedication, intelligence and physical exertion. Most rowers are up and on the water by 5:30 each morning, and national team athletes work out three times a day for ninety minutes to two hours each time. Even high-school rowers must put on a lot of kilometres if they wish to race successfully. Annelise Hall says she rows about twenty hours a week during racing season. "Rowing improves my life because of the exercise and because it makes me good at managing my time," she says. "I wake up at 4:30 to go rowing, then school from 8:00 to 2:30. After school I go home, do my homework, eat dinner, and I'm back on the water by 6:30."

Marnie McBean, double-gold winner in Barcelona and winner of silver in the women's single at the '93 World

*Members of the Calgary Rowing Club sculling on the Canmore Reservoir, Alberta.*

*Jack Coughlan, boatbuilder, Hudson Boat Works, Komoka, Ontario.*

*Medal presenters at the Universiade Games.*

Championships, says that rowers at every level of the sport make sacrifices: "I'm now coaching university athletes, and those people devote all their spare time to rowing. Commitment for most competitive rowers is high, but sometimes they forget about the fun they're having. Recreational rowers are the opposite; occasionally they're having so much fun, they forget about the hard work."

McBean says that good rowers have a certain maturity, recognizing the pleasure but also remembering what she calls the business of rowing: "When I began rowing, someone told me that in every stroke there are a hundred and sixty-eight things you can do wrong. Now I disagree; there are more. I have a mental checklist with about a hundred things on it—watch hand levels, power with the legs, good body posture, and so on. I try to get through the list with as many 'yeses' as possible; as soon as I get a 'no,' I'm in trouble. You have to have a dedication to the thought process. Ironically, that almost has to be thrown out the window when you're really pulling."

People begin rowing in numerous ways. I got involved at the Don Rowing Club in Mississauga, where my sister, Danielle, was rowing at the time. Marnie McBean became interested after she saw a movie about rowing and a television commercial featuring a rower: "I just looked up the Argonaut club in the phone book, went down and joined."

Mel Laforme got started in the sport as a high-school student in 1968: "I was just back from picking tobacco, which I did every summer and which gave me pretty strong wrists. Some kids were arm wrestling, and one of them kept beating everybody. Finally, they convinced me to participate, and I put him down. I was skinny and he was big, but because I had some wrist technique, some guys from the rowing team said I had to join them. I thought it was fabulous. We got up every day at 4:30, went down to the Leander Boat Club [in Hamilton], and rowed on the bay, then headed off to school. Around the school, people thought we were crazy to get up so early.

*Crew rowing on the Trent Canal.*

"I didn't want to stand out, I just wanted to be a part of something because I wasn't confident about myself. In rowing, you can contribute, and when you do well, you all do well together. A lot of people need that kind of experience."

Most major centres in Canada have a rowing club, so the sport is fairly accessible. If you're interested, investigate your local club, high-school, college or university rowing team. It's a great activity for fitness, as well as making friends. As Marilyn Copland, a director of the Victoria City Rowing Club and a masters rower, says, "It's an incredibly rewarding experience; I've found serenity, peace and exercise. And the great thing is, anyone can do it. It's truly a sport for all ages."

Former Rowing Canada president Sam Craig is equally certain that rowing has much to offer: "Rowing is one of the few sports, if not the only one, in which the sum of the parts is greater than the whole. Everyone works absolutely simultaneously, and no one goes into it to make money—they do it for love. It's difficult to explain the attraction of the sport; I feel I've taken far more out of rowing than I've put into it. But it's like anything else in life—you can't dance around the periphery if you want to get the most out of it."

*Preparing to take a boat out of the Credit River at the Don Rowing Club, Port Credit, Ontario.*

# TRAINING

*It takes a few years and a lot of work to build an eight. As we used to say, "You've got to row every day and twice on Sunday."*
—Claude Saunders, Chair of Royal Canadian Henley Regatta

A familiar expression claims that death and taxes are the only two things in life that can't be avoided, but for the competitive rower there's a third. Training is an aspect of rowing that rowers traditionally have a love-hate relationship with. And most have something to say about how it has affected them. Lorne Loomer, one of three novices in a coxless four that took gold in the 1956 Olympics, is certain about the role of training in his crew's success: "The first race we won by seven lengths, and the semi-final by ten. We won the final by five and a half lengths, although we almost sank at the start—our oars were going everywhere—and we were dead last by a thousand metres." Loomer speaks carefully, and there's modesty in his voice when he states that the win seems unique from his perspective today.

But he insists the victory had more to do with the crew's training than anything else. "We always had a time trial at the end of each row, morning and night," he explains. "We were given thirty seconds head-start on the eight, and occasionally, as we got toward the end of our training, we came across the finish line before them. This made Frank [Read] so furious he just turned us around, took us out to the line and demanded the whole thing all over again. But that was what made us more than what four people should have been."

Loomer remembers that every morning at five o'clock Read would walk down the stairs of the clubhouse, expecting to see his crews on the water and the coach boat engine running. "He'd step into his boat and off we'd go. That never varied; he had such total self-discipline. I think with leadership so positive and training so advanced for the time, we were fortunate. In relation to today, our training was probably quite primitive, but he made us put in more miles than anyone else. We may not have been a pretty crew, but after spending so much time on the water we were really able to move the boat."

Primitive is probably too strong a word to illustrate the difference between the regimen of forty years ago and that of today. Theo Dubois, who has been rowing in Winnipeg since 1926, agrees that training has changed, especially with certification programs for coaches: "I was trained strong on technique, now there's more concern on strength than on getting technique down. At one time you could tell by the way a crew rowed what club they were from. Today the sports federation and the Canadian Coaching Association have made the stroke more or less uniform across the country."

The trick of training hard is diversity. Certainly, the present approach with national team athletes is to have them feel that their environment varies. Kirsten Barnes, winner of two gold medals in Barcelona, says that's why her crews changed location about every two weeks in the summer of 1992. "Otherwise you get stale," she says. "With us it was train, race; train, race; train, race—right up to the Olympics. But I enjoy training. I like sweating; I like going out and just working hard. If I'm lifting weights, doing leg extensions or something, I start feeling that natural *up*, which helps me push myself to do another set."

*National team men's eight training on Elk Lake.*

In general, training for the national team provides a much more intense routine than any other level of rowing. Wendy Wiebe, who won gold in women's lightweight doubles at the 1993 World Championships, describes national team training as pretty gruelling: "We rowed three times a day, every day, or twice on the water and a workout with weights. We put on a lot of mileage, although the amount varied, depending on the cycle. We had one killer cycle over about ten days where we rowed thirty-six to forty kilometres each day, but on average we did about thirty to thirty-six Ks daily. For me this was a big change, because before that I'd only been doing two workouts per day. It was a noticeable increase."

Sometimes rowers work to the point where their hands are torn with blisters, their arms ache, and they feel so tired they couldn't possibly swing the oar back into the water. But if they keep going they reach a level at which they feel almost super-human. When that happens to me, I imagine I could easily keep up with the men's pairs (faster boats than a single). A surge of energy washes over me and I believe that no one can get past me. It's a kind of confidence that comes to athletes from extending themselves in training.

During training, athletes obviously do much more than accumulate miles. This is the time to focus on technique or overcoming bad rowing habits. Different boats can present distinctive challenges to rowers. Wendy Wiebe explains that one of the things she and her partner, Colleen Miller, had to concentrate on in training was holding the finish in: "After the catch, when you put your blade into the water, you want to keep it in as long as possible—you don't want to wash the blade out too soon." This is especially important in lightweight rowing, in which the rowers can't weigh more than 57 kilograms each. "You can only be so strong," Wiebe adds, "so you want to get the maximum power from each stroke." It's the kind of thing rowers spend a lot of time trying to master.

Besides its repetitive nature, training has several other unlovable aspects. For one thing, I'm not fond of cold weather, so on those chilly mornings in the fall and early spring when the air feels refrigerated, I find it tough to climb in my boat and lace my feet into the icy pair of

*National team member Darren Barber displays his hard-worked hands at the Elk Lake training facility.*

sneakers attached to the stretcher. I also find that during the months I'm really training hard, I can't do much else because I'm simply too tired in the evenings. At those times I miss having the energy to socialize, help around the house or start a project. Ironically, on my days off I feel guilty because I'm not training—I'm so accustomed to that process.

Other rowers may find problems with different facets of training. Annelise Hall, a young British Columbia rower, says she dislikes off-season training (winter keeps most Canadian rowers off the water for almost half the year). Usually, during this time rowers stay in shape by working out with weights or spending time on an ergometer—a kind of rowing machine often found in fitness centres and used to simulate the mechanics of rowing. "Dryland training has got to be the worst part," Hall says. "Pulling an erg is really boring; there's no rush, because you can't feel the water. Everything that's best about rowing is missing."

But I don't want to give the impression that training has no pleasures. There are benefits besides the obvious ones. When I'm training, I find I forget about the rest of the world. It's a time for reflection, a release from the chaos of life. After a while, other things begin to blur and I become

*When I started I thought it was hell. It was spring and we'd get going at five in the morning. It was cold and it rained a lot. I remember being entirely unco-ordinated. I just didn't have the hang of it. When you're new to rowing, you don't have an image of what doing it right is; you have nothing to measure yourself against. You can go through the rowing motions, but you're not technically refined. All you want to do is keep rowing.*

—Carol Latimer, member of winning eight at the 1990 Royal Canadian Henley

*Henley practice run in early morning fog.*

*National team women's eight coxswain Leslie Thompson and Rick Cawley (with megaphone) on Elk Lake.*

certain that putting the blades into the water, making a good stroke and feeling the boat move over the surface, is what's truly important, not all the complications of meeting deadlines or who'll pick up who after work. It's something so simple, yet so meaningful. And the physical rewards add to the attraction. I enjoy feeling strong and fit. I believe I get a lot of my energy from rowing, even though it's tough physical work. Training is a recipe for feeling youthful and alive.

Nancy Storrs, a rower who coaches at both high-school and national team levels, feels her own training affects the work she does with athletes: "Rowing on a daily basis is good for my coaching because I can sense the things I'm talking about. I can come up with different strategies— new words, new feelings. In coaching, I emphasize the technical stuff as a means to be more efficient, to be faster without more physical effort. As far as I'm concerned, everybody's going to train hard, especially at the national level, but the gains rowers can make by becoming smoother or increasing efficiency will eventually result in that extra second or two they'll need.

"With high-school athletes I see growth over the season in confidence, commitment, teamwork and self-perspective in terms of why they row. It's funny, they often begin to feel rowing is more important than school work, and if they have to take an erg test, they worry about it all day. That's when I remind them they're here for school and the rowing is meant to be fun. I want them to enjoy it and get a sense of the whole sport, not just focus on their eight or their four. Sometimes I get them to row in different boats than they normally do, because I want them to know what that's like."

To train without a coach is extremely difficult. As well as helping with technique, a coach can reinforce athletes' conviction that all the work is worthwhile. Brenda Backer, who won a bronze medal in the 1990 World Championships in Tasmania, actually coached herself and her rowing

*Rowing under the bridge at Trent University.*

*Olympic gold medalist Marnie McBean training on Fanshawe Lake, London, Ontario.*

partner in women's doubles for a year. "I really thought that was going to be the answer, because I'd had so many bad coaches," Backer says. "Now, even though I'm proud we made it through that year, I still can't believe we did it on our own. After that experience I realize the importance of having a coach. The coach is for fine-tuning performance. You get to the point where you're so mentally exhausted from the training you can't see or feel things properly; you start to lose sight of what's important.

"The coach also has to be someone who's strong enough to give you emotional support when you feel like you're falling apart. But it's hard to find a coach who'll listen. Some automatically assume that because they're giving you a training program, you will fit into their slot. Each athlete is an individual, and each will train slightly differently. When you say, 'Look, my heart rate has been about one-ninety every morning this past week; something's wrong,' you don't want to be told to get out there and do another twenty K."

Claude Saunders, a veteran rower who has been inducted to Canada's Sports Hall of Fame and who presently chairs the Royal Canadian Henley Regatta, agrees that coaches have to be sensitive to their athletes during training: "You need a coach who can listen to various complaints, and so on, then weld in a crew one idea of rowing." He cites two other keys to successful training: variation, to counter the boredom of routine, and, at least in an eight-oared boat, having a crew member who's a bit of a comic and can keep the rowers' spirits up. "Aside from that," he adds, "you have to train a lot; mileage makes the difference."

Athletes who row at the national level find that their training changes in more ways than simply duration and intensity. At this level, fitness alone isn't enough. They can't get by with just working hard, they also have to pay close attention to technique. For example, rowers might concentrate on developing an efficient rhythm to keep from rushing the slide—moving forward for the next stroke too quickly. If they row at too high a rate without good slide control, they become winded before their muscles grow tired.

For me, training means fifteen to eighteen workouts per week, each of which is about two hours in duration. I try to set weekly or monthly objectives and focus on specific aspects of my rowing. I might concentrate on the release, improving how my oars come out of the water, and attempt to reduce recovery time, how long it takes me to move back into position for the catch. As well, for each workout I set certain goals. I often do what rowers call time pieces—a series of short bursts, basically the equivalent of interval training for runners. As part of a 20-K workout, I might focus on doing three pieces of 4 kilometres each at a high intensity and within a certain

*A six-member women's crew prepares for a workout on Quidi Vidi Lake, Newfoundland, the night before the regatta.*

*Training inside the Winnipeg Rowing Club.*

*The latest fixed-seat boats for the St. John's Regatta were built by Hudson Boat Works.*

amount of time. This is challenging and breaks down the training session. Another time, I'll do a series of pieces in which I go full out for one minute, then rest for one minute, repeating this twelve to fifteen times. This is a short but intense workout technique that raises the heart rate.

I also feel it's important to mix an element of competitiveness into training. For example, in my single I'll race the double, with a thirty-second lead. As the double, with two rowers, is a faster boat than the single, this kind of match-up means I really have to push myself. It's reminiscent of Lorne Loomer's story about his four racing against the eight.

I find that my mind tends to wander on long workouts. After ninety minutes of straight rowing—catch, pull, release, feather the blades, recovery, and back to the catch again—I sometimes realize I've lost my focus and have begun to think about a phone call

*Oars hanging in the South Niagara Rowing Club boathouse, Welland, Ontario.*

I need to make or a presentation I have to give. When this happens, I devise what could be called concentration games. By forcing myself to think only about how I'm using my legs over the next 500 or 1,000 metres, for example, I'm able to block out the distracting thoughts.

But generally, training still affords the pleasure of concentrating on only the present moment. When I work hard I'm simply aware of myself and the boat beside me, forgetting about the rest of the world. When I'm not working hard I notice it, because it's too easy for everyday worries to creep back in.

I believe in the value of hard work. If you persevere at something, you'll get results. It's certainly true in rowing. But working and training hard also means addressing the mental aspects of the sport. Athletes must train themselves to want to win, to be in control of their bodies and their minds. I used to think that physical training was everything. Now I realize it's only the bread-and-butter essential. A rower can't accomplish anything without putting in the hours on the water, adding up the strokes. But altogether, training must address physical condition, technique and mentality. Claude Saunders recalls that his coach Jim Rice once said, "I tell my boys to get out in front, stay there and don't get tired. I would have been a world champion, but I got tired." Saunders adds, "What really determines success is mental attitude and determination."

This kind of determination and discipline is perhaps a large part of the reason for Canadian rowers' current successes in international competition. Sam Craig, founder and president of Toronto's Hanlan Boat Club, explains, "It comes down to a hard work ethic. There's no royal road to conditioning, no pill or machine that can do it for you. Perseverance and hard work—our rowing teams assume these things. The prize may not go to the best looking, but almost inevitably, it goes to the one who's worked the hardest."

*Rower and coach Owen Sawler with his son Bob.*

# COACHING

*There are always some who think it's brute strength. They tug and jerk and pull, and all they do is disturb the run of the boat.*
*But rowing is like ballet dancing—if it's carried out properly, you can't see the work being done.*
—Frank Read, national team coach from the early 1950s to mid-1960s

The yellow fibreglass crew shell moves across the dark water as eight rowers work individually yet in unison, focussed on the task of keeping up with each other. The early morning air is calm and cool; an overcast October sky holds no suggestion of warmth. Two oar lengths off their port side and a few metres behind, in the shell's light wash, a small aluminum motorboat follows. This is the coach boat, and the man in it, holding a black Kellerman digital stopwatch, shouts encouragement to the crew: "That's it. Keep tapping the boat along. Focus on the feel."

The rowers are aware of the chill in the air, but as they work they are immune to it. Their coach, however, seems oblivious to the weather. His concentration is on the crew— the movement of body and blades, the rhythmic co-ordination of eight oars in one boat, the fastest of all the rowing configurations. "Okay," he shouts, glancing at the watch, "let's pick up the pace in three. One. Two. Three." The rowers increase their stroke, the boat gains speed, and the man in the coach boat smiles to himself at the smoothness of the transition.

But what about the transition that put him in the coach boat in the first place? What drew him, like so many other men and women, to this calling? Much as in any sport, the path to becoming a coach is different for each individual. And as Mike Spracklen, one of the coaches for the Canadian national team that rowed in the 1992 Olympics, puts it, "Coaching is not a career; it's a way you choose to live your life."

For Jack Nicholson, who has been a national team coach on and off for more than fifteen years, the decision followed years of rowing and then boatbuilding. Nicholson never rowed at the international level, because he wasn't big enough and there was no lightweight category then. "But after rowing boats for a long time," he says, "I decided I wanted to try building them." Nicholson was the St. Catharines club boatman, doing all the repairs on the shells there, from 1953 to '58. "When I was building boats I got to know everything about them." Nicholson learned things such as which materials last longest, or why a rounder hull might make for a faster boat. He mastered the rowing-world mystique of setting the riggers—how a high or low pitch affects the angle of the blade entering the water, and which position might be best for a particular athlete.

"I also got to talk to all the coaches at the club. I'd talk rowing with them, the whys and wherefores, and I picked up a lot about technique and strategy. Besides, once you become a boatman, everybody thinks you know everything there is to know about rowing." Because rowing shells are fairly fragile, and setting the boat is so finicky— one change can throw everything off—most rowers are reluctant to change anything. Consequently, boatbuilders are considered the shamans of the sport. Nicholson's undying fascination with the way things work, combined with his boatbuilder's knowledge of materials and the insight he had gained from talking to various coaches, put him in a good position to begin coaching.

Nicholson first worked with high-school crews, applying what he had learned from talking to coaches, as well as

*Coach rigs a boat for a race the next day, Ridley College boathouse, St. Catharines, Ontario.*

from his personal experience. "In the seven or eight years I rowed," he explains, "I only once had the same coach for two years in a row. I benefitted from this because I was able to use the good points I'd gained from each of them." Nicholson is always open to learning more about technique, rigging, physiology—whatever he can share with athletes to improve their rowing—and went on to coach the quad that in 1985 won Canada's first gold medal in world championship men's sculling.

The late Frank Read's choice was made in 1949 when the University of British Columbia asked him to take on the coaching of the UBC crews. Read, who was a successful businessman and owner of three hotels at the time, saw this as a challenge to build a crew from scratch. "I had rowed for about four years back in the '30s," Read remembered. "When I took on the coaching job at UBC, I used

34

common sense. I studied the mechanics of rowing and then had to find out how to lead the boys to make them do more than they thought they could do." In fact, his crews did remarkably well at the 1956 Olympics, winning silver in the eight and gold in the four. At Tokyo, in 1964, his coxless pair's win was Canada's only gold medal of the games.

These days, many of the coaches in Canada study at the National Coaching Institute in Victoria, where the programs are so successful, according to Sam Craig, that they are copied around the world. Craig, a past president of the Canadian Amateur Rowing Association and founder of Toronto's Hanlan Boat Club, says everyone who attends the institute must already have achieved coaching level three, usually through provincial sport organizations. For rowing, level four involves working with a squad of national team coaches for a year. Participants study topics ranging from nutrition and site preparation to dealing with time-zone changes. All national team coaches, he says, must complete level four.

*Seats, Vancouver Rowing Club.*

Clearly, coaching rowers is a demanding commitment that requires a huge amount of time, for, as Read pointed out, good coaches won't ask any more of their rowers than they themselves are willing to do. That means being up at 4:00 AM to be out in the coach boat by 5:00, even on frosty autumn mornings. It means being back again in the evening, after a day at work (since most coaches are unpaid or receive only a token honorarium). It means weekends and holidays spent training or at regattas. A way of life, as Spracklen says. And despite all the time

invested, coaches don't get the same opportunities to experience the physical release of racing and the joys of winning that their crews do. Everybody assumes the coach is always motivated, says Spracklen, but coaches need some kind of encouragement, too. That motivation may come from watching enthusiastic, hard-working athletes gain something from their coach, make changes in how they are rowing, and achieve results.

But from the coach's perspective, there are other rewards. Nancy Storrs is one of the relatively few women coaches in Canada. She has coached athletes from high-school to national team level. Storrs was born in the United States, competed in the 1976 Olympics for the U.S., and now lives and coaches in St. Catharines. She says she enjoys working with high-school kids because she can have a positive effect on them and appreciates their excitement: "I'm not ultra-demanding of them. I want them to enjoy themselves, get a really good sense of rowing, and do it because they want to. This year I had kids who had never tried a team sport before. When they won the Canadian high-school rowing championship, they were in tears as they came in to the dock. One girl was crying and smiling and leaping out of the boat. That kind of reaction means something; that's what keeps me excited."

Jack Nicholson agrees: "To take young athletes and watch them develop gives me a sense of personal gratification. And you don't realize how much you influence some people as a coach. On a questionnaire we once gave some of the kids about their participation in sports, a boy wrote

*Brentwood College crew at the Canadian High School Championships.*

*National team coach Mike Spracklen with the men's eight on Elk Lake.*

that rowing taught him there was nothing he couldn't do, if he really wanted to do it. That kid eventually became a doctor."

In a sense, coaching keeps you young. When you're working with young people you develop an empathy with them, and the age differences between you almost drop away. "Coaches will feel young to the extent that they can put themselves in the athletes' shoes, " claims Cameron Harvey, who won a bronze in lightweight doubles at the 1986 World Championships and has coached at the club level. "When coaches feel the same nervousness and excitement as their athletes, that sets up a connection."

But aside from this appreciation of the athletes' enthusiasm, Harvey acknowledges other benefits: "The reward of teaching. If you have an image or vision in your mind of what you want to teach somebody, and you can do that successfully—seeing the results in a race won or a technique mastered—it's very rewarding. And then there's the

respect of your peers if you're able to bring along athletes and have them succeed in regattas."

No single ingredient can be identified as the thing that makes a good coach. Although I have had several fine coaches, I feel Mike Spracklen embodies many of the qualities I would associate with high-calibre coaching. What strikes me most about him is that he is a true professional. He is completely dedicated to discovering what makes a good rower. He also has a lot of patience. When he (or any coach) sees an athlete continue to make the same mistakes, it may seem the obvious and simple thing to do is to point this out and then have the rower change. But this isn't always the case. Spracklen understands the difficulty of making a change, the physiology involved as well as the psychology. When he explains how to do something differently, his rowers understand, and by following his suggestions, increase their speed. This gives him a great deal of credibility.

For example, before I worked with Spracklen, I'd

*Argonaut Rowing Club members with medals at the Royal Canadian Henley Regatta.*

always felt more comfortable keeping my oars close to the water. He pointed out that in rough water the blades would hit the tops of the waves and slow the boat down. Initially, taking the blades further out of the water made the boat feel unstable, but Mike would time me and show me that I was going faster. Over and over I trusted what he said, and that ultimately the results would prove him right.

I also feel Spracklen had confidence in me and my personal racing psychology. He knew I simply needed to work on certain aspects of my rowing, such as establish-

ing a good rhythm. He also knew that I needed to develop self-confidence. Knowing that he felt this assurance, that he didn't peg me as a good rower or a bad rower, definitely added to my self-confidence. This kind of supportive approach is another aspect of a good coach, and one that I have felt from several others I've worked with. It's important for athletes to feel respected by their coaches. Rowers are often mature athletes (the general competitive range is from twenty to thirty-two years of age) and consequently need to be treated as adults. They want to be listened to rather than always told what to do; to have

*Coaching at dawn, Vancouver, British Columbia.*

a chance to explain what they are feeling rather than just to hear what the coach thinks. Most successful coaches treat their rowers with respect, acknowledging that they know something about their own bodies and what they're doing.

Carol Latimer, who rows with Toronto's Argonaut Rowing Club and was a member of the women's eight that won at the Royal Canadian Henley in 1990, agrees that attitude towards the rowers goes a long way in determining the effectiveness of a coach. "The better coaches are very patient, constructively critical and don't treat you like a child," she says. "I've been very lucky with the coaches I've had. As for good ones, it always comes down to their commitment to the art of coaching. They want to develop talent, help you learn to be a better rower. And as they try to move you toward objectives—the Henley or whatever—they set training goals in co-operation with their athletes." Latimer also understands that from a coach's point of view, it's not easy to maintain a sensitivity to the rowers while organizing and directing them (in an eight you have nine people, counting the coxswain, to bring together).

A sense of mutual esteem is something many rowers

*Roger Jackson, 1964 Olympic gold medalist in the Men's Pair, is seen here at the University of Calgary.*

will tell you they look for in a coach. Cameron Harvey says, "The best coach is one athletes respect because he or she has a strong vision of how a good crew should work, or how to bring out the best in a sculler. And this has to be done in line with the accepted leading techniques at the time, not an attitude of 'I've got the answer, so don't listen to anyone else because this worked for me and it's the best way.'" He explains that it's a balance between staying open to new ideas and being able to stick fairly closely to what they believe works. "If someone on a crew questions a decision," he adds, "coaches have to be able to defend themselves competently, not just intimidate the rowers. It also definitely makes a difference if the coach knows what the athlete is feeling at various stages of the stroke or various stages of a race."

Harvey also feels it's not enough simply to be a good technical coach—to know the stroke inside out, or how best to put the blade in the water and how best to take it out. Coaches must be able to motivate their crews. "It's not a question of just drawing a diagram and saying, 'This is it,'" he insists. "They have to be able to communicate the idea simply and get the rowers excited about it. And

*I remember at a regatta in London, Ontario, some men from the military establishment there wanted to try rowing. One coach, George Flattering, had them out in the boat. When he shouted, "Easy all," which means stop, they kept going. So he shouted, "Let her run," which also means stop. They still didn't stop. Finally, he hollered, "For Christ's sake, halt." Luckily they understood that time or they would have hit the pier.*

—Claude Saunders, Chair of Royal Canadian Henley

though everybody may have their own way of motivating themselves as individuals, as a crew, rowers have to feel some sort of unity. Usually, it's the coach who shapes that spirit. So a good coach is a technician, a motivator and a communicator."

An effective level of communication between coach and athlete is not easy to achieve. I didn't really understand the role of creativity in coaching until I started training with Mike Spracklen. Now, I believe that coaching is an incredibly creative activity. One aspect is the ability to verbalize criticism. For example, a coach might talk to a rower about swinging her body forward, how she must be able to feel the weight shift. Anyone can tell the athlete what to do, but a good coach gives you an idea of how it's going to feel and how it will affect the entire stroke. Sometimes an athlete is told hundreds of times to change something, and even though he makes an honest effort, he can't make the change. At this point, coaches must think of a way to describe what they want, to get the athlete to correct an ingrained habit.

Much of the time, athletes are not conscious of this taking place. They simply appreciate a particular coach's facility for helping them. As Carol Latimer says, "A coach has to figure out how to translate what he or she is thinking to the athlete in a way in which they'll be able to grasp the concept. Often, 'quicker at the catch' won't do it. It's such a simple phrase and you ought to be able to do it, but it doesn't mean anything perceptually." Good coaches, she explains, are able to go beyond the key phrases and get their rowers to feel things, to get in touch with their physical selves in ways that work for them as individuals.

The skills of coaching don't come easy and, of course, don't come to everyone. And, since most coaches volunteer their time, especially at the high-school or club level, it's often tough for them to juggle the rest of their lives and

*Masters rower Marilyn Copland out for a row on Elk Lake.*

*Vancouver Rowing Club's men's eight at the start of their race at the Royal Canadian Henley.*

their coaching. As well as a solid understanding of the sport, it takes a combination of ability and intuition to be outstanding. "There are lots of people who know something about rowing," said Frank Read, "but not many who can lead their rowers. There are plenty of different styles, so if you start talking techniques you can get into a lot of arguments. In the end, it's the results that count."

But it's not easy to get those results. Other elements of rowing and racing also come into play in the job of coaching. Jack Nicholson talks about the difficulties of always being able to give the rowers the motivation they need: "The toughest thing about coaching is when you know you've got a good crew, but you're also aware there are two other boats likely to beat you unless they have a real bad day. You've still got to try to inspire your crew to win, but at the same time be realistic about it and leave them an out. That's where I'm always concerned to set enough objectives. You can lose a race and still come out of it with something. So you leave the door open for them to win, but if they lose you've got to say, 'Well, we tried this and it

*Pre-race talk in the boat bay at the Royal Canadian Henley.*

didn't work. Let's go back home and figure out what will work.' I've seen too many coaches who just focus on winning and nothing else."

There are additional difficulties for women. All the coaches I've had have been men, largely because there are very few women coaches in Canada, and only one or two at the national team level. This might be related to the time commitment necessary to be a coach; despite changing role perceptions, it's still more difficult for women to be away from their homes and families than for men. Women generally bear greater responsibility in raising children and caring for their families.

It may also be that coaching doesn't hold the same appeal for women. I have no ambition to become a national team coach. (I have an enormous respect for coaches and their commitment, but because I've sacrificed so fully to be an athlete, I'm not prepared to give up more to meet the demands of coaching.) Nancy Storrs says she began with the

*Detail of boat with dew.*

national team almost by chance when the women's double at the time insisted on a female coach. Even at this level, she sometimes feels she doesn't have the same credibility as her male colleagues. But she tries not to see it as an obstacle and hopes her results with the rowers will speak for themselves. These days, more and more women are getting into coaching, and as their numbers increase, it will become easier for other women to get involved.

One of the biggest problems with coaching in Canada is that few of the clubs are actually able to pay their coaches. As Jack Nicholson says, "People used to ask me what's wrong with Canadian rowing, and I'd say,

'Nothing that money wouldn't fix.' We could win a lot more medals if we had sufficient support and money spent wisely. Out of all the sports, Canada has got the most for its dollars spent on rowing. But the general public doesn't believe in coaching as a profession. A lot of good coaches leave because there's no money in it. You can't afford to raise a family and be involved in coaching. There's a hell of a lot of divorced coaches; it's that demanding." He says the National Coaching Institute turns out fine rowing coaches, but then they can't get a job in Canada. "Why are we training them for other countries?" he asks.

Perhaps this situation will change as rowing continues to gain a higher profile here. In the meantime, there's no doubt that the individuals who devote themselves to coaching contribute a huge amount to the sport. Coaches have helped me not only to become a better athlete, but also to become a more mature and better person—the two are closely linked. My coaches have been people I've looked up to and sought advice from. One of my first coaches, Fred Loek, was someone I would often go to when I had a problem. In 1986 I almost left rowing because of a back injury and some other matters, but Loek encouraged me to stay. He reminded me how much I love the sport, how much pleasure there is in simply rowing.

Even with the success in rowing that I've had, I still feel I need someone to watch me and tell me what they see, whether it's something I want to hear or not. It's the coach's perspective which provides that pair of eyes.

*A member of the North Star Rowing Club rows under the highway bridge on Lake Banook, Dartmouth, Nova Scotia.*

# SINGLE SCULLING

*The great thing about the single is that you can strengthen that part of yourself which is often very frightening—being alone and doing things
on your own, without the support of other people around you. To do well in the single, it's only you.
If you can actually push yourself to the limit and come up with a good race, it's a great feeling.*
—Brenda Backer, winner of bronze in the 1990 World Championships

On a glorious summer afternoon in London, Ontario, the flowers are in full bloom and the willows that line the banks of the Thames River seem to reach toward the smooth-running water. A sleek, single rowing shell emerges from around a sharp bend in the river and heads downstream towards the bridge that marks the familiar turnaround point. The sculler feels the warm July sun on her arms and legs, and enjoys the easy movement of her boat as it slips across the water. The scull is so fast and weightless, she has the illusion that her body is gliding over the surface without a boat. Stroke follows stroke as her oars grasp the river and move the shell along. The blades enter the water at a measured angle and speed, precise and rhythmic with the mesmerizing repetition of the rower's movements.

The boat progresses down the river, and to anyone watching, the oars appear to be only gently tapping the water. But the rower's aching muscles and burning lungs contradict this picture of apparent ease. As she moves toward her goal, her legs are tight with fatigue. At the moment her blades grip the water, her legs drive the seat towards the bow of the boat, pushing it forward. To move the shell quickly, she drives her legs hard, using all her strength in an attempt to get the most out of the boat. In a long workout such as this, she knows she mustn't pull with wild abandon, but with power and precision. As she nears the turn, she begins to count strokes.

When she reaches the bridge, the rower rests her blades lightly on the water and allows her boat to drift gently to a stop. She breathes deeply and wipes the sweat from her upper lip against the sleeve of her T-shirt. Turning in her seat to look around her, she takes in the warm stillness and smiles. Despite the hard work, rowing alone is a beautiful and peaceful activity. On a day like this, she feels a connection with the world around her and imagines she could row forever along this river.

The image of a solitary rower moving over a placid stretch of water on a summer day brings to mind many of the appealing qualities of single sculling. The silence of one boat propelled by one person; that effort translated directly into the movement of the shell as it skims across the water; the independence that comes from this singular pursuit—these are some of the magical elements that draw athletes to the single scull.

Sam Craig, founder of Toronto's Hanlan Boat Club, is a singles rower who began in a crew boat. Business travel commitments made the scheduling of crew rowing difficult to manage, so he switched to a single (although he says he hasn't rowed much in the past few years because of an injury). "When you're in a single," he says, "and you catch a morning when the water is absolutely flat, with the sun reflecting off the buildings downtown, it's therapeutic."

He's not alone in his love of singles rowing. Although their reasons may not all be the same, many rowers speak

*A lone sculler returns his oars to the Ottawa Rowing Club boathouse.*

ardently of their experiences in this type of boat. Brenda Backer, who has rowed on Canada's national team in both the double and single, says, "I have a passion for sculling because it's even—you're doing the same motion with both sides of your body. When I was in sweep, I rowed in pain all the time because of the unevenness of it. So, as much as I enjoyed sweep for the team aspect, I also hated it. When I started sculling I loved that I could push myself so hard and not hurt my back. I never wanted to go back to sweep after that."

For some rowers, choosing the single is a matter of convenience—in an individual sport, there are no work timetables to co-ordinate and no waiting around for anyone else. Bruce Trewin, captain of the Vancouver Rowing Club, says he has become addicted to sculling, partly for this reason. "Coming from an ex-runner's perspective, the fact that you can work on your own suits me," he explains. "You can set your own schedule, the level you want to train at, and there's no question that the success or failure comes down to you. There's no one else to blame."

But a lot of people enjoy crew rowing. Having a connection with each other, team rowers psyche each other up. Whether they do poorly or well, they share the experience. On the practical side, many people wouldn't row every day unless others were waiting for them. And some rowers see no appeal in winning

*National team member John Wallace prepares for a workout on Elk Lake.*

by themselves; they like the group excitement, celebrating together afterwards—it's all part of the sport. Working effectively on a team is a challenge. Also, crew boats are so fast and powerful, some athletes don't feel the same satisfaction in a single.

Still, many others prefer the individual aspect of single sculling, which crew rowing doesn't satisfy. World championship bronze medal winner Cameron Harvey says, "I prefer single sculling to team rowing because of the independence of it and the autonomy you have when you're out there. When you push harder you see the direct results of what you're doing, and that goes for racing, a hard workout or nice long row on a beautiful day. You're on your own and you get such a direct feeling of your impact on the boat through the blades in the water. For me, you can't beat that feeling."

Single sculling requires a skill that can take years to master, partly because the boat is long and thin, and therefore unstable. It's very easy to tip a single—the first time you get into one, you feel as if you're balanced on a string and that any motion could easily put you in the water. Besides presenting this precariousness, sculling seems more technical to me than sweep rowing, basically because you have two oars to think about. However, Marnie McBean, who won a silver in the '93 World Championships in women's singles, feels that each form has its own technicalities: "It's a trade-

off. The bladework in a single is more difficult, but it's harder to get the timing right in a pair. The way I see it, rowing is like walking a tightrope. In a single, the balance pole is in both your hands; in a pair, one-half the pole is in your partner's hands. In the single, you actually have more control."

When rowing the single, there's no one else to follow. In all other boats, athletes sit behind or in front of someone, which makes timing and synchronization of movement paramount. In a team boat, the coach must have a strong idea of an effective stroke, then have the crew work together to achieve it. Athletes with different body shapes and sizes ideally adapt to a uniform technique. As national team coach Jack Nicholson says, "Sometimes it doesn't matter so much what the crew is doing as long as they're all doing it together." The single sculler has no one to coordinate movements with and can therefore develop a technique that best suits his or her physique. For example, a reduced catch angle—how the blade enters the water—may suit an individual's body mechanics, and in the single, this characteristic doesn't affect anybody else.

On the other hand, too much time spent in the single can lead to idiosyncratic rowing techniques and can make it extremely difficult to adapt to team rowing. Sometimes single scullers can stubbornly refuse to change old habits. They may feel that the style they've been using for years works, so why should they change in a crew boat. This type of thinking works against team rowing, where synchronous movement and thinking are crucial.

Kay Worthington, a national team rower since 1978, and I had proven ourselves as competent international scullers before the Olympic games in Seoul, Korea. We had both placed fourth in the world in single sculls, and on paper our combination looked like a powerful one. But

*Rob Marland training for the national team on the Trent Canal, Peterborough, Ontario, 1990.*

*Sculling along the St. Lawrence Canal, Thunder Bay, Ontario.*

despite our commitment and drive, we couldn't make the boat move quickly—largely, I believe, because we were both holding onto old ideas about what had been effective for us in the single. We were unable to blend physically and psychologically with each other.

There are other difficulties that might arise out of choosing singles rowing. For one thing, being by yourself all the time can be the most enjoyable and, at the same time, most problematic aspect of the sport. When the skies are cloudy and motivation ebbs, it's easy to find a reason not to row. There's no one depending on you and no one to spur you on. Even if the sculler trains in a group, it's always against, rather than with, other people. The many miles it takes to become a proficient single sculler can be lonely ones. And when you always row alone, you tend to become overly self-critical and demanding of yourself.

*I recall rowing singles at the Canadian Henley, years ago in Port Dalhousie. The water was horrendous there, sort of a giant sewer.*
*As I came up to the dock, a fish jumped into the cockpit of my boat. When I asked my coach, who was standing on the dock,*
*why it would do that, he said, "The fish would rather be in there than in that water."*
—Moe Cody, Secretary of the Nova Scotia Rowing Association

*A recreational sculler rows down the Saint John River at Fredericton, New Brunswick.*

This can have a negative effect on your rowing. Ultimately, you're out there alone each day with no one to support you on the bad days, and no one to share the feeling of the boat when everything's going great.

But not all scullers row alone. There are three sculling disciplines: single, double and quadruple, or quad. Each of these boat's oars are slightly shorter and thinner than sweep oars. And although in all sculling boats the athletes hold two blades, each discipline is quite different. A good single rower does not necessarily make a good quad rower, and vice versa. In the quad the motions are faster than in the single, and the sense of timing must be perfect, because it's a team effort. Each boat also demands a different psychological approach in competition, so some rowers are better suited to one boat than another.

Creating a successful sculling team can be tricky. Often the athletes spend a great deal of their time in singles and combine late in the season to form their crew boat. The rowers must adapt to each other and accept a team approach in which no person is better than any of the others and the common goal is more important than an individual one.

Internationally, Canada has had moderate success in team sculling. Among these were the double of Janice Mason and Lisa Roy, who won a bronze at the 1981 World Championships. In 1987 Mason and Heather Hatten clobbered their competitors in lightweight doubles at the World Championships to win the gold with a six-second margin. And in '93 Wendy Wiebe and Colleen Miller took gold in the same category.

*Derek Porter (left) and Mike Forgeron, silver medal winners in the Universiade Games Men's Quad, stand for the anthem.*

*Silken Laumann training on Elk Lake.*

Perhaps one of the most successful crews in Canada's sculling history was made up of Paul Douma, Doug Hamilton, Mel Laforme and Bob Mills. Their various career and family commitments prevented them from training together during the week, but they got together on the Henley course each weekend to train in the quad. This crew formed a magical combination that won the 1985 World Championships in Belgium and continued to win medals for the next few years that they were together. "The majority of our practice was in singles," says Laforme, "but when we got into the quad, it seemed that everything was fantastic. Each of us was that much sharper, making sure that if there was going to be a good practice, it would be in that quad, because we had so few opportunities to get together. We took roles in the crew—Paul as the young guy who got most of the abuse, Bob as the calming influence, and so on. Some crews do well because they're all alike or fit into a pattern. We were all different but felt the whole dynamic could accommodate four different roles."

Without a doubt, one of the greatest attractions of the single is the freedom it allows a rower. When the water is flat and the sun is shining, the single sculler can row with ten minutes' notice. I love the single because there's nobody to organize, nothing to arrange, no being early or late. A short bicycle ride to the boathouse and a few minutes spent carrying my shell down to the lake, and I'm rowing. Once on the water the workout is as short or as long as I want to make it. An extra mile is a pleasure granted whenever motivation is high—in the single, no one else determines when your practice is over. I've always been able to train as much as I wanted, something that has definitely been an asset to my rowing career.

Occasionally, sweep rowers will switch to sculling. Derek Porter, who won a gold medal in Barcelona in the

*National team sculling blades on the dock at the Elk Lake, British Columbia, training facility.*

men's eight, took up the single shortly after the Olympics, and a year later won the gold in singles at the '93 World Championships: "It generally takes a longer time to convert from sweep to sculling. There are a lot of changes to make. Not so much in the gross movements, which are more or less the same, but mostly the blade work. You have to get the blades down into the water and lock on more efficiently. It also takes a while to get the feel and confidence in the boat—it's way more tippy than the eight.

"I felt I almost had to take a step down. I knew I had to do a lot of rebuilding, and going into the '93 competition, I didn't think I had a good shot at a medal. In fact, everyone expected I'd have a longer haul from sweep to sculling. But it's been a good progression for me."

Another rower who's been successful in sweep rowing, winning gold in both the women's pair and eight at Barcelona, Marnie McBean also moved into the single, to take silver at the '93 World Championships. For McBean, sculling is nothing new, as she's had her own single since 1988: "I focussed on sweep but I used the single as a sideline, to train on my own." Even so, changing her focus from one to the other, presented her with a challenge. "I went from being very effective at sweep to inefficient in the single. But having had the experience of learning to sweep made it easier to switch. I remembered the steps I'd have to go through."

Other crew athletes also row in a single as a training aid, but have no plans to compete in it. Marilyn Campbell, who won a silver medal in the women's four at the 1984 Olympics, is known as being a great team player, but she also enjoys the single. "My strengths don't lie in being a single sculler," she says. "I basically taught myself to scull in the mid-80s. I was sort of a fifth wheel because there were five of us who were traditional sweep rowers working together. I was a bit older than the others, and my

*A Kingston Rowing Club sculler removing a single from Lake Ontario.*

*Training in single sculls on Burnaby Lake, British Columbia.*

*Two scullers row toward the docks as a thunderstorm moves in on the Welland Canal.*

boyfriend at the time had a single. I just got in the boat and pulled, so I don't think I was a pretty sculler. I got workouts in, kept myself in shape and raced everyone on the lake. I really like the sense of power and exhilaration from pulling on one oar, but when you lock on in sculling—your blade's in there nicely and you've got your back into it—that's a great feeling, too. I don't know if you can compare the two; they both have their joys."

Racing is one of the most exciting aspects of rowing a single, but also one of the most intimidating. I've heard many rowers say that they love single sculling, but they're afraid of racing. Sitting in the starting gates in a single for the first time can be a frightening experience—there's nobody else in the boat with you to give you a pat on the back or help calm your nerves. Some rowers need the motivation of others, to know the crew is depending on them. Inevitably, in the single, the realization dawns that the responsibility for the race is yours alone. As well, racing in a single exposes the athlete's weaknesses for all to see. If you row poorly, there's no one else to blame. Many people who have never raced the single fear that they'll stop when it starts to hurt (as it always does) because there's nobody counting on them. However, this is probably more fear than likelihood, since I have rarely seen an athlete stop rowing during a race.

*Silken Laumann finishes the Women's Single at the 1991 Speed Orders on the Welland Canal.*

And when a race does go well, the single sculler has the satisfaction of knowing it was all his or her own doing. There are no grey areas about timing or meshing of styles. Singles rowers are accountable for their own results.

To my mind, because of the closeness to the boat, being in a single takes rowers closest to the beauty of rowing. There are fewer variables than with a crew, and it's so quiet—no other oars clunking—you can focus more on what you're doing.

It's also challenging, because it's possible to go out one day and suddenly feel as if you've never rowed before. If you take the boat out a few hours later, everything comes back to you. You learn a technique—how to improve your slide or maximize the power from your legs—and then struggle to keep what you've learned. And even when you've mastered a particular point, you may still feel that it's almost on the verge of eluding you. This is part of the paradox of sculling—it can be demanding, yet also incredibly appealing.

Whether for recreation or competition, the single scull more clearly captures the aesthetic of rowing than any other boat. It also allows the freedom to row by yourself and control the amount you train and race. For all these reasons, and because it suits my personality best, the single will always be my favourite boat. Certainly, for me, the best part of rowing is the quiet beauty of sculling alone on a warm summer day.

*Stepping into the boat at the Thunder Bay Rowing Club.*

# TEAMWORK

*Rowing provides a social community that can be intense and difficult at times, but you share something with these people that you'll never share with anyone else again in your life. That history, those memories, are never going to be lost.*
—Cameron Harvey, winner of bronze in Lightweight Doubles at the 1986 World Championships

The Barcelona sun beats down on the Olympic regatta site where the half-dozen finalists in men's coxed eights are all pulling hard out of the starting gate, no crew an obvious leader up to the first 500 metres. The Canadian team, dressed in red and white with an oar-crossed maple leaf logo on their shirts, are among the pack but ready to begin their move for front position. The coxswain shouts, "Push hard; drive with the legs. Here we go!" and the eight rowers work to make their blades enter the water simultaneously. Muscles strain as each drives his oars through the water. The stroke rate is high at this point—forty-two per minute. Each man is determined to make the boat move faster. And the way they work together—balance, timing, a meshing of eight bodies into a single entity—resembles the workings of an elaborate machine.

By the first quarter of a 2,000-metre race, the human body has built up a lot of lactic acid in the muscle tissue, and the brain begins to suggest taking it easy. But the Canadian rowers have a plan. They have decided to ignore the mind's insistence and really push at the 500. "The day before the race, we held a crew meeting and discussed strategy," says Rob Marland, a rower in the eight. "We made some changes in the boat, like switching the stroke rower. As a group we made a commitment to win. We knew we could win a medal, but we didn't want to come second or third—we wanted the gold. We decided not to play it safe, but to go full out."

With 750 metres to go, the Canadian eight was in front, but only by half a boat length. At the beginning of the final 500, the Germans and Romanians were both keeping up the pressure. But, as the Canadian team had planned, the cox called their mark and the rowers began their final drive to the finish. "We won the race right there," says Marland. "The boat came alive—it was electric. That was definitely the most dynamic experience of my life. I still get goosebumps when I think about it. The Romanians were gaining on us, but at two thousand metres the race was over and we got there first."

I don't imagine any of the athletes in that crew would dispute that teamwork is what won that race. On the medal podium, they hugged and congratulated each other, rejoicing in their success as a crew—nine individuals who worked together toward a common goal.

In crew rowing, perhaps more than any other sport, each individual's performance depends on the others in the boat. When a team rows well, responding together under pressure, it's a beautiful thing to watch. Each athlete almost anticipates the movements of the others. In a sense, they appear to be mentally linked. In most team sports, an individual can stand out and be recognized even if the team is mediocre, but in a rowing crew, an athlete is only as good as the rest of the team. Everyone in the crew moves together in a game of follow-the-leader—the stroke rower, who sets the pace. If one person doesn't get his oar

*Edmonton Rowing Club intermediate women's crew rowing on the North Saskatchewan River.*

out of the water fast enough, the entire crew must stop, since it's impossible to move effectively when not working as a full crew.

"What happened in Barcelona was just the tip of the iceberg," explains Marland. "Three years of hard work and dedication made us strong as individuals and as a group. In 1990 we came third at a regatta in San Diego, then took silver at the World Championships. In the spring of '91 we raced the Germans, who had been the best, and we smoked them. We thought we'd win the World that year, but came second. However, the margins weren't that great. We also did some racing early in '92, so by the Olympics we had gone through an incredible journey as a group."

Members of a rowing crew must develop complete trust and respect for each other. After you've rowed with someone for a long time, you learn their idiosyncrasies, the way they do things. There may be moments when certain behaviour bothers you, but ultimately each team member must believe that the others are all working equally as hard as (or harder than) they are. "Respect for each other is really important," says Kirsten Barnes, who won gold in both the women's eight and coxless four at Barcelona. "Problems can show up with lateness, rowers not being prepared or organized. Courtesy issues, in a lot of ways. But if there's a problem, I'd choose to solve it via the coxswain or coach, because I wouldn't want to jeopardize that relationship or friendship—that respect. In a crew, you're all equal."

*Two exhausted competitors await the results of a photo finish at the Canadian High School Championships. They won as part of the senior women's eight.*

This feeling of regard among teammates is important in all crew boats. However, Marilyn Campbell, who won a silver medal in the women's four in the 1984 Olympics, believes it may be even more critical in pairs and doubles. "When I compare the eight, the four and the pair, I prefer the pair because it's only the two of you, and you can really develop a strong relationship. You've got to have respect on and off the water, otherwise you can't row together. The bottom line for me is that it doesn't matter who's in the boat with you as long as you respect each other."

Crew rowers often talk about the thrill of teamwork, of feeling like they are extensions of the people in front of or behind them. Coaches sometimes ask them to imagine there are strings connecting each rower in the crew to the others. They must know their crewmates so well they can anticipate their movements. In a crew, if you wait for the stroke rower to put her blade in the water before you do the same, it will be too late.

Working together as a team is a vital aspect of achieving success in crew rowing. Wendy Wiebe, who won gold with Colleen Miller in lightweight women's doubles at the 1993 World Championships, understands the necessity and subtleties of co-operation: "Teamwork is everything in the double. Two people slamming through the water is not going to work; it's more of a finesse boat. It's important that we do each motion together, in the same way at the same time.

"In a race you're pulling hard the whole way, but technique is still important. For example, making sure you're

*St. Catharines masters crew celebrates a victory in the 500 Metre Dash at the Royal Canadian Henley.*

*A Calgary Rowing Club crew celebrates their victory in the Men's Four at the Royal Canadian Henley.*

both using your legs at the beginning of the stroke, not in the middle; or having a similar emphasis in applying power during the stroke—these things are critical. And having Colleen as a partner certainly helped. She's such a positive person to race with."

I enjoy the feeling of moving my own boat and being in control of everything, but some people don't see the joy in that. In a single there's nobody to talk to, compare notes with or blame if things go wrong. Most people like to see what they can do on their own, but basically rowing is a team sport. For the majority of rowers, much of the pleasure of rowing comes from learning to work and think as part of a team. Cameron Harvey, who won a bronze in lightweight doubles at the 1986 World Championships, says, "I just love the connection of the body to the boat to the water—the unity of that motion. When you sweep you get that feeling, but you're also part of something, and that's the appeal of crew rowing. When you get a boat moving in complete synchronicity with eight other people, that's an overwhelming feeling. You're contributing to something that's bigger than you are.

"The first time I did any crew rowing was in '85, in the lightweight eight. That was the fastest boat I'd ever been in. I remember when we raced the U.S. crew. Before the race we had a team meeting in the back of the boathouse. There was a sense of being with eight other guys who each had the same feelings of anticipation, anxiety, tension and unity—of having a purpose. It's a tremendous sensation to participate so actively."

In his administrative capacity, Claude Saunders, chair of the Royal Canadian Henley, sees a lot of rowing crews. Saunders also rowed in the eight chosen to represent Canada at the 1940 Olympics (which didn't take place because of the Second World War). "Rowing in an eight doesn't take long to learn," he says, "but learning to make a boat really move takes timing. There are eight different personalities in a boat, and it's a job to get them doing the same thing at the same time with maximum effort. But through this, rowers gain a valuable lesson in life about getting along with other people."

Certainly, there are many benefits to being part of a crew. You can always count on having others to motivate you on days when nothing seems to be going right, or you simply feel uninspired. For both competitive and recreational rowers, it often helps to know that someone is waiting for you at the dock at 5:30 in the morning, when you don't feel like getting out of bed. As well, camaraderie and long-lasting friendships are elements of rowing that any rower will eagerly cite as part of the sport's appeal. Lorne Loomer, who rowed on the Golden Four in the 1956 Olympics, counts fellowship as one of the most vital aspects in solidifying that crew during the months of training: "So many times our four sank out in Coal Harbour. After we were picked up by pleasure craft and had the shell towed home, you could see the four of us, with our thick woollen socks soaking wet, walking down Georgia Street to the clubhouse. There was a wonderful feeling of we're-all-in-this-together, and there's a lot of power in that."

Wendy Wiebe first rowed in crew boats but switched to the single for a while before returning to the double. She appreciates being back in a boat with another athlete: "It's nice to row with someone else, and sometimes it's easier. If one of you is having a bad day, the other can pick her up. You never have a giggling fit in a single, but in a double, sometimes everything you see seems hilarious." Wiebe also recognizes the motivation that teammates provide during a race, when there are moments that a rower's body experiences acute pain and fatigue. "In a crew, you never want to let your partners down," she says. "Sometimes that's what keeps you going."

Working as a team can be a positive and rewarding experience, but developing good teamwork doesn't come easily. Being in a crew, rowing day in and day out with the

*Throwing the coxy into the pond after winning the Royal Canadian Henley.*

*Members of the Winston Churchill crew celebrate their victory in the Lightweight event at the Canadian High School Championships.*

*Washing down a boat before a race at the 1990 Canadian High School Championships.*

same people, occasionally creates problems between crew members. Kirsten Barnes explains that rowers have to separate the crew's common goal from a particular personality trait someone on the team might have: "There are times when you get tired of the others and their idiosyncrasies. I just walk away from those moments and don't let them bother me. I'd see something happening that I knew would annoy me, so I'd just excuse myself from the situation and appreciate that it's simply a quality of the other person. We're all out there for the same reasons but we're all different; everyone's going to have their own approach to achieving those goals."

As coxswain, Terry Paul of the men's eight that rowed in Barcelona feels it's his responsibility to deal with the interpersonal problems that arise on a crew. "It's all part of being a good coxswain and a mature athlete," he says. "There's always something that will piss people off, especially when rowers are extremely tired. I used to take things personally when someone would yell at me or somebody would be consistently late. But I got to the point where I could recognize what was happening and not so much try to remedy it, but deflect the situation a bit. I never ignore issues, and always try to be sensitive to whether it's best

*Oar hanging in a boat bay at the Delta Deas Rowing Club, Delta, British Columbia.*

to be serious or be a goofball and keep things light. When something happens—say one guy is always late—I try to play it down. If it's consistently one or two guys, the rest of the crew can lose confidence in them. They might be perceived as incompetent or less committed. I make sure the others don't start to feel they can't rely on these guys, so we don't go on the line with any doubts or concerns."

From the point of view of a single sculler, there are other drawbacks to team rowing. For one thing, it's much more difficult to schedule workouts when nine people are involved. And if you're the crew member who wants to train the hardest, you're always waiting for the others in order to get on the water. But sometimes I miss the sense of support and unity that crew rowers have.

Tensions, personality differences and scheduling all must be resolved if a crew is to have success. The ability to think and act like a unit is essential, and individual rowers must somehow mesh. If one member of a crew leans a certain way in the boat, the others must accommodate even that tendency. Rob Marland says that crew members learn to adjust to each other physically by putting on a lot of miles together: "It's a process of adapting to each other. You

*It seems, from the crews I've seen, it's not so much getting the best people that's important; it's how they work together, how they mentally complement each other. Sometimes I'm amazed when a good rower doesn't make a boat go faster.*

*But that's the magic—the personalities, and the physical weaknesses and strengths combined. That's why watching a crew row together can be so beautiful.*

*—Mel Laforme, former Olympic rower and present high-school coach*

*The McGill men's crew rows past spectators at the Head of the Trent.*

learn to contribute and not disturb the boat. Our eight rowed in pairs together and switched partners, so each of us went through the whole group. That way we learned what each of the others was like."

Marland adds that the meshing of the different personalities can take time: "In our crew, the guys came from all across the country. Some of us were married and some weren't. And there was an age spread of about six years. However, as a group we were all there to achieve a common goal, and although individual differ-ences are magnified in stressful situations, we learned to overcome them."

Kirsten Barnes also acknowledges the importance of working to achieve a group cohesiveness: "We spent four years on moving together, and all the components that go into that. But what [coach] Al Morrow wanted to see was a uniform crew, with everyone and everything exactly the same—our bodies, our bladework, everything."

Coaches encourage crew members to work with and support each other. "It's a crew effort," said the late Frank

*Cooling down at the finish of the Royal Canadian Henley Regatta.*

*Crews in the sun at the NCAA Rowing Championships in Cincinnati, Ohio.*

Read, coach of the Canadian Olympic rowers in the 1950s and early '60s. "That's what makes it so beautiful to watch. It's similar to a team effort, but you're all in one boat. You've all got to do exactly the same thing at the same time—there's no individual achievement as such—you've got to co-ordinate. There's no sense pulling twice as hard as the person in front of you. It doesn't work that way."

Successful crews must combine all the basics of team rowing—technique, training, teamwork and unity. But I've seen a lot of races won by crews that are often not the most talented. However, they seem to have something unique as a group. Certainly there can be other elements involved in building a crew that works well together. Marilyn Campbell, whose four won a silver medal in the 1984

Olympics, says that having something in common (besides a devotion to rowing) can solidify a crew: "The team I was on in '84 had all gone through a struggle—the loss of a parent or someone else close. This means we developed some emotional toughness which we transferred to the sport. That allowed us to go one step farther. The hard work was always there, but this other helped us get to the top. You need something deep to create a strong base, and it's either there or it's not. Also, communication is important. When I think back to the crews I've been most successful with, we had a strong communication link."

Perhaps rowers realize the most significant reward of crew rowing when they win a race. The personal satisfaction of winning in a single may be greater than in a team boat, but there's nobody to share it with. To win as a team means being able to look into the face of the person next to you and know you are experiencing something together that no one outside your boat can know.

Campbell still remembers rowing in a regatta in San Diego as a member of her university team. "It was our first time down there," she explains. "One of our coach's strengths was in analyzing and interpreting the field, telling us exactly where our strengths were. He pegged it perfectly, told us what to do, and we did it. We won over Washington—not by a lot—but the thrill of it working and all coming together is something I've never forgotten. It was quite powerful.

"After crossing the finish line in a crew boat, you experience two levels. There's the personal part, because you've had to push yourself. But you also have the people in front of and behind you. I think in a crew, and particularly in an eight, you develop a special rapport with the others. I guess you break yourself into little pieces to join in a stronger chain—that's your support base."

The relationships that develop among rowers often last a lifetime. This is particularly true of friendships built between crew members. These people see a side of each other that is unadorned; no matter who you are, in a boat you are just another blade. There are few areas in life in which people get to know one another so intimately. And some rowers continue to row together well beyond their competitive years, or remain in the sport in other capacities, such as coaching or managing. Marilyn Campbell, for example, has created a high-school rowing program in Victoria that involves about two hundred athletes each season.

Rob Marland is grateful for what he gained through his participation on the national team eight. "We're all friends for life," he says. "I'm a rich person from having worked in this group. The life skills I gained are incredible."

Shortly after Barcelona, Marland's team was invited to a celebration in Ottawa for Canada's Olympic athletes. "At one point, our crew got away from everyone else," says Marland. "We sat down in a small room with beers and went around the table, discussing the race. It was three months later, but it was the first chance we'd had to really talk about it or reflect on it as a group. And that's a moment I'll always cherish."

*Canadian women's quad celebrating a gold medal performance at the Universiade Games.*

*Thunder Bay (Fort William) Club rowers in front of their boathouse.*

# CLUB ROWING

*Rowing is an unforgiving sport. Basically, you're always rowing toward yourself.*
—Nikos Apostolopoulos, Vancouver Rowing Club

Rowers are often told to push from their legs, that the basic drive and power of their stroke begins there. To draw an analogy from this, I would say that the club rowing programs are the legs of Canadian rowing. "Club rowing is the foundation and strength of Canadian rowing, and always has been," says Sam Craig, founder of Toronto's Hanlan Boat Club and a past president of Rowing Canada. "And we are among the very best rowing nations in the world."

Almost every rower in the country, including national team athletes, has a club association. The social aspects and competitive atmosphere of club rowing appeal to rowers of every skill level. It also offers an opportunity for people who may no longer get out on the water (or may never have) to maintain a connection with rowing in other capacities, as coaches, organizers and so on. There are about eighty clubs across the nation, from the St. John's Rowing Club in Newfoundland to the Victoria City Rowing Club in British Columbia. They sponsor everything from learn-to-row programs to national team training; from local and regional regattas to the Royal Canadian Henley—an annual event begun in the 1880s and now among the largest meets in North America.

Craig explains that even most high-school rowing is run by clubs, not the schools, and cites the example of Kingston, where he says seven or eight schools row out of the club. "And very few college rowing programs aren't run from the clubs," he says. "Upper Canada College has its own program but operates from the Hanlan club. They

use some of our equipment, and we use some of theirs."

Typically, rowers begin their careers in a high-school or college program. The first shell I ever stepped into—and promptly tipped—was a single (although I also dabbled in an eight for about a week) at the Don Rowing Club, in the novice training course. I was seventeen, and my older sister, Danielle, was already among a strong group of women rowing at the Mississauga, Ontario, club. Like most other girls my age, I was interested in boys and parties, but I knew I wanted to become an Olympic athlete. At first, rowing didn't attract me; it wasn't glamorous enough. But eventually, watching Danielle and other women at the club working at it and achieving success, the sport drew me in. And although these days I row out of Victoria City, I still have a lifetime membership in the Don club.

Moe Cody, secretary of the Nova Scotia Rowing Association and a member of the North Star Rowing Club in Dartmouth, says he started rowing in high school: "I grew up in Brockville, a small town with a rowing club. It was the only game in town if you didn't play baseball. The club offered a chance to tour—the Henley, Montréal, Buffalo, Philadelphia, the CNE regatta in Toronto. That was big travel in those days." Cody says that at the age of twenty-five, he became "disinvolved" with rowing for a few years, but returned to the boats when he moved to Nova Scotia. Now his participation is largely administrative, working with the provincial rowing organization, though he was chief rowing judge at the '93 Summer Games in Kamloops, British Columbia.

*Placentia Bay Rowing Club crew in Placentia Bay, Newfoundland.*

Long-term commitment at the club level is characteristic throughout the country, and is part of the strength of club rowing. As Cody says, "I feel I owe the sport a great deal. As a result of my achievements, I received an athletic scholarship, so I credit my education to rowing. Now I'm able to put something back in."

As well as school and competitive programs, the clubs offer various other categories of rowing to accommodate a wide range of interests. "There are now over three hundred casual rowers in St. Catharines alone," says Claude Saunders, chair of the Canadian Henley. Saunders has remained involved in rowing since the fall of 1931, when he joined Hamilton's Leander Boat Club. "In addition to the regular rowing programs, the City of Hamilton operates a recreational rowing course through the club for two weeks in the summer. It's purely recreational; these people are not interested in competition."

Saunders also notes that every club has a masters group—for rowers who are beyond the age of international rowing but still wish to row competitively. "The number of masters rowers has doubled in the last few years," he adds. "This includes both men and women. The twenty-seven to forty-year-old group is very competitive, but the forty to sixty-five-year-olds generally just enjoy taking part."

Marilyn Copland, a director at the Victoria City Rowing Club, where approximately one in six of the members are masters rowers, calls them a precious commodity in any club. "They serve on the executive, work as fundrais-

*The Outer Cove Rowing Club crew, with Jim Hibbs in stroke, train on Quidi Vidi Lake, at St. John's, Newfoundland, before the regatta.*

ers and donate money," she says. Copland ran the Canadian masters program in the late '80s. She explains that masters regattas are organized by age categories in five-year increments from twenty-seven to eighty. "Older rowers are given a handicap of one second per year difference over younger ones. We take the average age of the crew, excluding coxswain, and race over a thousand-metre course. And a competitive oarsperson must be at least one year out of the national team to compete in masters."

Copland says a national masters regatta is held each year in Canada, alternating between sites in the East and in the West. "But a lot of people can't afford the travel," she says, "so the rowing association is thinking they should have two regattas, one in the East and one in the West."

Rowers don't necessarily retire at sixty-five, however, as witnessed by individuals like Winnipeg's Theo Dubois, who still rows daily when the weather allows, and in masters regattas, although he's in his early eighties. "You can always go down to the club and row," he says. "You don't need to get a team together—just get in a boat, and once you're on the water you're already practising for an event."

Dubois, who was awarded the Lou Marsh trophy in 1941 as the outstanding Canadian athlete of the year, says he joined the Winnipeg Rowing Club in 1926 because his parents wanted to keep him off the streets. "When I started I was about the only one at the club who was from a working-class family. But the fees were reasonable then, and they still are."

Basically, anyone interested in rowing can join a club. "We offer learn-to-row programs, which are a fairly typical initiation to the sport, in early spring and summer," says Bruce Trewin, captain of the Vancouver Rowing Club. These are run as both day and evening programs, and each accommodates as many as sixteen people, ranging in age from twenty to sixty. "We start with an information session and safety course, then go on to the boats. Traditionally, rowers spend the first three or four rowing sessions on a barge which holds sixteen, then graduate to eights and eventually the smaller boats. There are ten lessons in all, which take about one month and give the participants the basics and an awareness of the sport. This is enough to go out on your own or with someone else, but it takes a year or more to really learn to row. During summer we provide some coaching and programs together with community centres and schools. We've even designed a program for blind athletes. Of course, we also run programs for community colleges, and now the majority of our competitive athletes come through these courses. We may get one competitive athlete for every fifty people who go through learn-to-row."

Although the commonalities in a sense unify the clubs, each region and each organization has its own distinguishing features. For instance, Moe Cody points out that in the Atlantic area, rowing has to compete with paddling: "A lot of people here who could be good rowers go into paddling instead. And to develop a truly strong base, we also need more clubs, boats and money. It's an expensive activity which requires major fundraising. There's not much government support for any sport which doesn't have a high level of participation. So we've been trying to involve more people, particularly through university programs. At Dalhousie we had one hundred and seventy-five rowers last year, and St. Francis Xavier University would like to start a program. But it's still a problem of how to get the

*A Peterborough Rowing Club crew on the Trent Canal.*

boats and money. We just completed a five-year plan which saw our athletes compete in the '93 Summer Games. Now we're developing another plan, but it's a painstakingly long process."

On the Prairies, as Theo Dubois explains, Winnipeg has long been the key rowing centre: "We were the first club here, then it spread to Regina, Calgary, Edmonton and Saskatoon. I remember back in the thirties, asking people in Edmonton why they weren't rowing on their river. They said they couldn't even paddle a canoe on it because of the sand banks. Well, they must have found somewhere to row, because they now have a fine rowing club there." According to Bill Sabey, Edmonton Rowing Club vice-president, the 125-member club was incorporated in 1974 and rows on the North Saskatchewan River in the city's west end.

Dubois says that rowing is strong on the Prairies and across the country these days: "The clubs here can barely keep up with the interest, especially since our crews did so well at the '92 Olympics. We've had to split up the days at the Winnipeg club because we don't have enough equipment. Anything that popularizes the sport to the degree Barcelona did means more clubs and more regattas. And there's nothing like competition to keep enthusiasm high."

Even the clubhouses have their own natures. Sam Craig describes the home of the Hanlan club as resembling an army Quonset hut: "It's basically a tin shed run for and by the athletes. Our only concession to the soft life is a Porta Potty." Craig says he founded the club in the early '70s when his son was in a high-school program at the Argonaut club, also in Toronto. "The club was going though a metamorphosis at the time and my son's program was having some difficulties, so I found some property with the help of the city, and the rowers themselves built our clubhouse."

This stands in stark contrast to places such as the domain of the Vancouver Rowing Club. Built in 1911, the

*Members of the Don Rowing Club rowing on Lake Ontario.*

*Masters rowers in front of the Leander Boat Club, Hamilton, Ontario.*

*Ned Pratt, winner of the 1932 Olympic bronze in the Men's Double, seen here at the Vancouver Rowing Club.*

three-level wood-frame structure looks out on Coal Harbour at the edge of Stanley Park. The building also houses a rugby club and a field hockey club. "The club is unusual," says Bruce Trewin, "because, although it began as only a rowing club, it grew into a multi-sport operation." The VRC has boat storage and launching facilities, men's and women's locker rooms, a bar, an entertainment room with a small stage, and several meeting rooms. One of these features trophies and other historical artifacts (including Ned Hanlan's gold-topped walking stick) proudly displayed against dark, wood-panelled walls. "It's a very comfortable building with a lot of history behind it," says Trewin.

Pride in one's club is a common feature of rowing, and every club has its rival. For example, the Don and Argonaut clubs are old adversaries. When I rowed at the Don club, a victory was always a little sweeter if we beat the Argos. However, these rivalries are kept on a very friendly level, never malicious, and people occasionally move from one club to another.

"There's actually a lot of co-operation among the different clubs," says Claude Saunders. "I remember some years ago going to a regatta in the U.S. I was hauling boats for several different clubs—Argonaut, Don, Leander—and

Bows of pairs at the Victoria City Rowing Club.

stopped at a service station. When the attendant learned I had other clubs' boats on my trailer, he was astonished. 'You pull other people's boats?' he asked. 'I thought you'd put holes in them.' I told him that in rowing, if we can help others, we do. We have a saying: 'After us, you come first.' And it's the same all around the world. In 1979 we went to Australia for the first world championship held outside Europe. You can't imagine the lengths they went to in order to find us a boat we were satisfied with."

The club rowing system is closely integrated with national team rowing. As Nancy Storrs says, "It's basically the intermediate step between high-school and international competition." Storrs, who coaches at both school and national levels, believes in the importance of club rowing to Canada's international performance. "I like the concept of having even more club rowing and more rowing in smaller centres," she says.

Bruce Trewin sees the club system as the most important element of rowing: "It's the base of the pyramid. No one goes on to competitive rowing unless they've been through a club program. And without this base, we would never have people moving up into the national program. Competitive people can't do the

Live your life extraordinarily. You shouldn't settle for anything mundane. Out here, rowing, I get to thinking about the really great things I want to try in life. When I'm off working nine to five, I don't have time to think about those things. It seems like the stuff inside of you that really sees and feels, goes to sleep. Rowing wakes you up.
—Jennifer Doey, double gold-medalist in the 1991 World Championships

*Rowing at sunrise on Lake Superior.*

legwork, too. So others, who don't row, for whatever reason, provide the foundation. Also, funding for the national team is based on the numbers involved in the sport."

At one time, selection for the national team was made from rowers who competed at the Royal Canadian Henley, but the process has changed. Theo Dubois remembers, "They used to row off in St. Catharines a year before the Olympics to see who would represent Canada. Now there's a different approach; they start building their teams five years ahead of time. The advantage is, they can pick the best oarspeople from clubs across the country."

Another important side of club rowing is its social environment. Rowers get to know each other well, working together each season towards common goals, such as competing in and winning regattas. For many, summer activity peaks at the Canadian Henley, held every August. Some people form friendships and associations within their club that will last throughout their lives. As Bruce Trewin points out, "There are a lot of club members who only get into a boat once or twice a year. What the club provides them is a broader social structure." Clubs hold dances and barbecues, bring in guest speakers, or simply provide a comfortable place to meet. "The social aspect of the club is where people get a feeling for the family of rowing—the sport's essence," says Trewin.

Although club rowing has many strengths, there are a few areas in which some participants would like to see improvement. One thing that would certainly make a difference in club rowing programs, especially in terms of competition, would be for clubs to have paid coaching

*Ian McFarland and Chris Flood stand on the end of the dock at the Kennebecasis Rowing Club, on the Saint John River.*

*Theo Dubois, 1941 Lou Marsh Trophy winner, looks through treasured photographs at his home in Winnipeg.*

*Members of the Saskatoon Rowing Club single sculling on the South Saskatchewan River.*

positions. Unfortunately, most clubs don't have the funds to do this, but the ones that do see a noticeable difference. For the past few years the Don Rowing Club has had a paid coach during the summer. This is a major step in providing the kind of continuity needed to maintain a top level of performance—at the club level, who's on top is based largely on the coaching.

Carol Latimer, a member of the Argonaut club, feels this lack of financial support for coaches is one of the biggest problems in rowing. "It's tough," she says, "because at the club level, coaches are out at 5:30 in the morning and have to go to work after that. It leads to a lot of turnover and a lack of consistency. We've got to develop a greater long-term vision. Maybe the clubs need to be run more like businesses, with the people who work there being paid.

But I don't know how that would work; obviously, it could get pretty expensive, which then raises questions of accessibility. There's no simple solution."

I too feel the club system needs to grow and develop in Canada; this is where everything starts, the basis of all rowing in the country. To ensure a strong future for the sport here, we need more clubs with solid programs and professional coaching. In the meantime, much of the strength continues to come from the high level of membership commitment and dedication. Also, as rowing relies on people putting something back into it, rowers seldom leave their clubs completely. Often, they serve on the executive or maintain some other connection, even if they're no longer rowing there. So long as this attitude remains, club rowing in Canada is certain to thrive.

*Brentwood College Invitational Regatta, Brentwood Bay, British Columbia.*

# RACE DAY

*To row from ahead and win is nice, but it's a little extra special when you come from behind and just row right through. When you win like that, you feel very powerful.*
—Marilyn Campbell, silver medal winner in Women's Four in the 1984 Olympics

The history of racing on water probably dates back to the day the second boat was launched. Competition is a major part of rowing—it's what you work for, the pay-off for the long, often tedious, hours of training. For me, it holds a bit of a contradiction. I find I wait and wait for the day of the race, and when it finally comes, I dread it because it's a test. The problem isn't a fear of failing the test, but controlling the exhilaration and nervousness. It all comes down to a period of about seven minutes, and then it's do or die; there's no second chance. So you have to work around the emotions and concentrate on doing your best. Ironically, these feelings are part of racing's attraction. Rowers who never race miss out on the incredible highs (and sometimes incredible lows) that come with the territory. There's no age limit to these feelings—everyone from kids to the oldest of rowers will admit to the intense excitement.

Regattas offer coaches and athletes an opportunity to show off their skills and test themselves against others. Since many rowers train on their own or without racing for six months at a stretch, they're eager for a chance to measure their progress. On regatta day, rowers dressed proudly in their team colours race to add a trophy to their clubhouse display case.

For many clubs in Canada, competitions are rare occasions because of the distances to be travelled. A club from Northern Ontario may only meet Southern Ontario clubs twice a year, and rowers from Regina, for example, face a six-hour drive to race in Winnipeg. Consequently, each encounter holds a lot of weight. Coaches look forward to regatta day as a chance to compare notes and share opinions and ideas. It's not uncommon to see two coaches from different clubs standing on the bank of the raceway, animatedly debating the fine points of rowing, such as whether a high rig, in which the boat is set so rowers pull high, is superior to a low rig, in which rowers pull the oars in lower.

A regatta is a scene of noisy activity—the energy and anxiety of the rowers almost tangible. "First call for novice women's four," an authoritative voice proclaims from the loudspeaker as athletes wipe down a hull or check the condition of their oarlocks. "Last call for masters men's singles." Long, sleek racing shells cradled on handmade, sawhorse-like stands, and multi-level boat trailers are scattered around the clubhouse yard. Eight men make their way solemnly to the water, carrying on their shoulders a boat designed for nine athletes, including coxswain, but which weighs only 95 kilograms—about the same as one of the rowers. A young woman adjusts the riggers on a double while her partner checks the seats on the slides. At the dock, a coxswain, standing a head shorter than the rest of his crew, shouts to be heard above the loudspeaker's announcements. "Up over your heads," he calls, "Ready. Roll. Push the boat up—and, into the water."

Canopied stalls, positioned near the spectators' bleachers, sell T-shirts, homemade cookies, lemonade and other treats. It's all happy chaos as athletes, coaches and supporters mix around the regatta site. Lining the banks of

*The start of the Head of Trent on the Trent Canal, Peterborough.*

the raceway, which is marked with fluorescent orange buoys, scores of rowing enthusiasts sit, chatting between races or standing with binoculars to see who is in the lead out of the starting gates. Parents, friends and others who simply enjoy the sport shout encouragement to their favourites. A grey-haired, ruddy-faced boating veteran instructs the young boy beside him to pay attention to the smoothness of the rowers' movement. "Winning is important," he says, "but watch the way these lads work together."

Whether done for pleasure or to make the national team, the experience of racing can be highly stressful. Even the most confident athletes feel the pressure of the competitive test. Putting yourself on the starting line means facing the risk of disappointing yourself (or even worse, others). "As a novice, I was terrified my slide would fall off," says Carol Latimer, a member of the women's eight that won at the Royal Canadian Henley in 1990. "I saw it happen to other people and it seemed to be the most embarrassing thing possible in life, other than catching a crab. I became paranoid that it might happen to me. You only have one race," she says, "and if something goes wrong, that's it. It's not the best three out of four." Catching a crab, or crabbing, happens when a crew rower doesn't get his or her oar out of the water fast enough. This can force a boat to stop, and may even pitch the crabbing rower into the water.

*Ian McMillan inside the St. Catharines boathouse, preparing for the championship race at the Royal Canadian Henley .*

Most of the anxiety rowers feel over racing hits before they even get to the starting gate. For me, the pressure begins to build a few days before a race. Although it happened more when I was younger, the adrenaline and excitement still sometimes make me sick to my stomach. When I wake up on the day of the race, the world seems unusual, so completely focussed. Until I'm sitting in my boat on the far side of the finish line, there's only one thing on my mind. No matter what happens before that, everything but those seven minutes of rowing seems insignificant.

I still remember my first race. I had learned to row in August, and I entered as a single at the Head of the Trent a month later. The course had a strong turn in it, and I was so worried I would tip in the rough water that my forearms seized up. But I kept going and actually won the novice category. One of my most vivid memories of that race is of a national team member who knew my sister, Danielle. As I rowed, I could hear him shouting from the bank, "Technique! Think about your technique." It was all I could do to keep pulling.

Once rowers are sitting in the starting gates, waiting for the gun to go off, the focus and anticipation they feel blocks out the rest of the world. Good athletes think about what it will take to give their best performance. Derek Porter, winner of gold at the '92 Olympics and the '93

World Championships, says this used to be the toughest part of the race for him. "You're actually waiting in the gates for a few minutes," he says. "Enough time to feel nervous and scared with the realization that you're going to have to push yourself over the limit. But recently, I feel calm and almost peaceful because I know how hard I've trained and because of the accomplishments of the past—especially in Barcelona."

Over the years I've gained confidence. I prepare myself in several ways because I never assume I will somehow just do everything right. I concentrate on what I must do to win the race and where my focus should be, planning how to pace myself at the beginning of the race or when to make my move in the final 500 metres. And I acknowledge that there will be pain. Racing has taught me that pain can catch an athlete by surprise, so it's important to anticipate it. It has also taught me that the feeling of pain doesn't matter. For example, at the '92 Olympic final I knew I would feel physically terrible after the race if I rowed full out, but I also knew I'd feel a lot worse if I didn't row to my potential. That race took a lot out of me. I was tired and slightly nauseous for a few days after, because I'd pushed myself so hard. However, I knew that I'd done my best and it was extremely satisfying.

Merely talking to most rowers about racing is enough to raise their heart rates, so it's important they try to remain calm in the starting gate. I've had to learn to consider the nervousness as something positive. The tension means you're ready and you care. A great coach knows the adrenaline is potentially useful and works with the athlete to channel it rather than shut it down. My coach, Mike Spracklen, never told me to ignore the nervousness; instead he helped me discover the benefits of this state. So I pay attention to my breathing and visualize the first five

*Upper Canada College crew at the start of a Canadian High School Championships race.*

*A sculler from the North Star Rowing Club puts his boat in Lake Banook, Dartmouth, Nova Scotia.*

or six strokes—quick and clean—in a sense memorizing what I'll do when the race begins.

The official Olympic rowing distance is 2,000 metres for both men and women (most regattas are held on a course of this length). Since the human body can't sprint the entire length, probably the ideal way to row a race is to keep a fairly even pace. What tends to happen, however, is that once the gun sounds, crews go full out for the first few hundred metres. Each crew tries to get an early psychological edge on its opponents. If a crew doesn't sprint hard the first 200 metres, it loses the pack and the advantage of having other crews racing alongside. At some point most rowers worry whether they'll be able to push themselves hard

enough. "Waiting for the starting gun can be nerve-wracking," says Wendy Wiebe, winner of gold in women's lightweight doubles at the '93 World Championships. "It's the only time in the race when you're not in control. I take deep breaths, stay loose and focus on something like keeping my blade in the water as long as possible. You can't be thinking two hundred metres ahead or you won't be able to do what you're supposed to do. When the race starts, I take it one stroke at a time."

Once the initial sprint is over, rowers must find an aggressive rhythm they can hold for the body of the race. Racing at any level is extremely demanding. After a few hundred metres, muscles begin to scream—you're asking

*Disappointment at the finish of the Senior Women's Double, Canadian High School Championships.*

*Two scullers almost tip their boat at the start of a Canadian High School Championships race.*

the body to keep sprinting when there's not enough oxygen available to them. This anaerobic state, the creating of an oxygen debt, can only be maintained for a short time because the heart rate is at its upper limit and unable to handle the workload. At this stage, a rower's motivation to continue must be high.

According to the coach of University of British Columbia crews in the '50s and early '60s, the late Frank Read, "Rowers have to learn to push back the fatigue barrier, to keep putting in more effort." If they are going to win, rowers will hurt, too. They have to force themselves beyond the first pain threshold, to the next one and the next. Each athlete is motivated by different things. Some want passionately to beat other rowers; some want to satisfy their own expectations. But it basically comes down to one thing, as Wendy Wiebe says: "We work so hard, dedicate so much time and effort, all to win."

Whatever the motivation, a crew will need something to get through the core of the race when the body tries to convince the mind to stop working so hard. Coxswains can make the difference at this point. Chosen partly for their light body weight, coxswains are in charge of steering the boat and shouting encouragement to urge the rowers on. They can see clearly where the crew is in relation to others, and during a race, act as surrogate coaches.

Terry Paul, coxswain on the men's eight that won gold in Barcelona, says of that race, "It seems to me we went through the first thousand [metres] really fast. I remember noticing we were still really moving and that we were ahead of the others. I was just thinking about keeping it on the boil at the thousand because I knew traditionally that's where our low was. Any time I felt we were coming off the edge I'd call something like, 'Punch the legs. Keep it going.' I tried to keep putting on little pushes all the way— three strokes or five strokes. And when I yelled something like, 'Keep attacking it,' I could feel the guys react." John Wallace, a rower in that crew, illustrates the relationship between rowers and coxswain: "Everyone was keyed in to Terry's voice. Near the end he said, 'There's only seven or eight strokes to go.' Whenever he says that, I believe him, because after so many workouts and races together, I know how accurate he is in counting strokes. I've never been able to figure out how a person could do that."

For a single sculler, the source of motivation during a race is obviously somewhat different. I focus on getting maximum performance from myself, on working myself harder and harder. I disregard any negative thoughts, such as how tired I am, or momentary doubts about my ability to win. I want to cross the finish line knowing I gave the race everything I had. I also don't want anyone to be better than me. If someone is beside me, I think, I'm just as capable as her to win; there's no reason I can't beat this person. Whenever I've been in head-on battles, stroke for stroke, I think of the other rower as simply a boat I've got to get past.

In Barcelona I was very focussed on giving my personal best. Rather than worrying about my competition, I tried to focus on rowing a great race. I thought about how hard I'd worked most of my life to be in that particular competition, and that I had to do it, then and there. Until the last 500 metres, I just tried to stay with the rest of the pack. For me that's really the point when I begin to key in to the other rowers. So, when we got near the finish and ahead of me I saw Anne Marden (silver medal winner for the U.S. in singles at both the '84 and '88 Olympics) my only thought was to push past her. Explode with the legs, move the arms out fast—this is what I was thinking. Everything was happening very quickly. I had put myself through so much to be there—years of struggle, the leg injury in Essen ten weeks earlier, and the subsequent hundred and fifty or more hours of physiotherapy—I just had to get the best out of myself. I kept thinking, Push, push, push. In the last 500 metres of any race, I'm almost blind with fatigue and can only think simple thoughts, such as,

*Weighing in for the Lightweight event at the Canadian High School Championships.*

*Coach Harry Parker helps his Harvard men's eight prepare for the 1991 Dash event in the Victoria Boat Race.*

*The Don Rowing Club lightweight women's crew nears the finish at the Royal Canadian Henley.*

*Kennebecasis Rowing Club crew at the start of a race during the Canadian Championships. The two baldheaded crew members were shaved as part of their initiation.*

Use your legs. If someone asked my age, I wouldn't be able to answer.

In this race it was peculiar that the harder I worked, the more energetic I felt. At the Olympics, much of the race is an internal struggle not to give in to the pain and exhaustion. Since my competitors always bring out the best in me, the other boats helped me to keep rowing hard. Anne Marden, by staying with me and sprinting for the finish, enabled me to achieve my goal of winning a medal—a concrete symbol of all I'd overcome. As a competitive athlete I've been trained to win, and being so close to winning a medal made it easy to find the inspiration I needed.

Many races are decided in the last 500 metres. Consequently, as rowers approach the finish line, they reach a point where they have to choose whether they want to win or not. Although they've built up a rhythm, they now have to break it and become even more aggressive to get through the last of the race. In my case, it's almost as if a switch flicks and I go into a kind of overdrive, because at this point the physical exhaustion is generally quite severe. I realize at that moment I have to make an absolute commitment to winning. All I think is, I'm going to do it. I can't leave any room in my mind for doubt, because that's all it would take to keep me from putting in the effort required.

Derek Porter says that over the course of the final at the '93 World Championships, the rowers changed positions about four times. However, at the final 300, he noticed he was losing by three-quarters of a length to the Czech Republic's Vaclav Chalupa. "There's always a lot of pain in the last few hundred metres," he says. "But when I saw him ahead of me, I thought, It's now or never, and just pumped up my rate." This remarkable effort led him to win by 1.5 seconds.

Athletes have many different reactions to winning a race. I'm usually glad it's over, and I seldom feel like

*The Ned Hanlan Trophy is awarded to the Men's Eight champions at the Royal Canadian Henley.*

*The start of a race at the U.S. Nationals in Indianapolis, Indiana.*

shouting. At first I might feel pride or satisfaction; it's later that I feel excited.

Kirsten Barnes, who rowed on two gold-winning crews in the '92 Olympics, knows what it's like to win an important race: "When we crossed the finish line in the four, I felt excitement and relief. Since '91 we'd won a lot of races, and there was no reason we couldn't win that one; we'd already beaten all those crews. But when it was over I was amazed that we'd actually done what we believed we could do."

The expectations rowers have of themselves and their performances can often be a key element in working toward their goals. Terry Paul says, "The best part about winning the gold medal was the anticipation of just how great it would be to win. That was what kept me going over the two years. That was my motivation."

When Colleen Miller and Wendy Wiebe won at the World Championships, they also felt rewarded for their years of training. "It's hard to pinpoint the feeling," Wiebe says. "I've been trying to win for a long time, although I've come third a lot. I think the best part of the regatta came after hearing the beep when we crossed the line and realizing we were first, that I wasn't

*Oars in the rafters of the North Star Rowing Club, Dartmouth, Nova Scotia.*

in some kind of a daze. It was a pretty gruelling race—my lungs and legs were in agony—but it hurts worse when you lose."

For some, the key to winning may seem elusive. But Claude Saunders, chair of the Canadian Henley, says, "The one who wins the race is the one who's best. In the rowing world there's a continuing source of controversy over styles, shells and equipment—what makes a boat move fastest; it goes on and on. But all the arguments are settled on the water. Jim Rice, my coach in the 1930s, used to say, 'I've seen a lot of fast horses but no fast carriages,' Ultimately, it's not the design of the boat, but the people in it."

Competition may be fierce at a regatta, but it's usually friendly. The same athletes who are rivals on the water often can be seen enjoying a beer together after the race. Rowers are known for congratulating their opposition, shaking hands or hugging each other on the medal podium. In rowing, there's a saying: "Respect your competition, for they are what will make you better." The importance of racing to rowers can perhaps be seen in a similar light. They may dread regattas or they may love them, but ultimately, racing is where they will truly show their best.

*In the final stage of a race, my brain shuts off, so I don't remember much about the last few hundred metres. After the race I was in a bit of a daze, slumped over my oars; it took me five seconds to get back to consciousness. When I realized I'd won, I felt happy, but mostly surprised.*

—Derek Porter, on his '93 World Championships win in Men's Singles

*Men's national team training at Elk Lake.*

# NATIONAL TEAM ROWING

*I'm hard-pressed to think of someone harmed by rowing. The injuries are minimal, the benefits, optimal; the fellowship is first-class and the memories last a long time—incidentally, the old boats get faster as more time passes.*
—Sam Craig, founder of Toronto's Hanlan Boat Club

In many ways, it's the stereotypical Canadian scene: a tree-rimmed lake, calm and quiet, as the morning mist rises from its surface. A family of mallard ducks travels in a group near the shore, while trout rise to snatch insect breakfasts, leaving evidence of their presence in widening circles on the flat water. You can almost imagine a fur-laden canoe paddling out of the fog. But this picture is not what it appears to be. On the highway that passes the lake only 50 metres away, a steady stream of traffic hurries to make the early ferry to the mainland or the eight o'clock whistle at work in Victoria. This is Elk Lake on Vancouver Island, the west-coast home of Canada's national rowing team. And if any boat comes forging out of the mist here, it's likely to hold eight powerful rowers responding to their coxswain's encouraging voice.

Victoria, British Columbia, and London, Ontario, are the two main centres for Canadian national-level rowing, with clubs such as St. Catharines, Montréal, McGill and Brock University also running strong programs that feed the national team. In the past, the team was separated into three divisions: men, women and lightweights, with the men and women having different head coaches—Mike Spracklen and Al Morrow, respectively. Lightweight was distinct because, although this category has been included in the world championships since 1975, these athletes will not appear in their first Olympic regatta until 1996.

However, beginning in May '93, all national team rowers now come under the umbrella of a single head coach, Brian Richardson.

"Rowing Canada changed the team's structure to create a true head coach position when Mike Spracklen returned to the U.S.," Richardson explains, "and Al Morrow has moved into athlete development." Richardson is from Australia, where he worked as a national team coach since 1986. "For the next few years, my job is primarily team building," he says. Richardson's main focus will be on preparation for the '96 Olympics.

To represent Canada at international competitions and the Olympic games is an honour many young rowers strive for. National team members were once chosen from among those competing at the Royal Canadian Henley, but the selection process has changed. Today there is a regatta called the Speed Orders, held every spring on the Welland Canal in Ontario. Athletes row in either a single or a pair, and this opportunity to show how fast you can be is open to anyone in the country.

My entry to the team came in 1983. I'd been rowing since the previous fall and had just won the Canadian high-school championship in women's singles. When my coach, Fred Loek, suggested I try the Speed Orders, I was intimidated by the idea of rowing against what I felt was a group of incredible athletes. I was so frightened that when

the starting gun began the first race, I sprinted in sheer terror and won the heat. The next day, I came first again, and eventually won the semi-finals. During each race, I was all over the course and didn't know what I was doing, but I pulled hard.

On the last day, at the beginning of the finals, my seat popped off the rails. No one had told me that in the first 100 metres of an event, if you have an equipment problem, you can raise your hand and stop the race. So I spent some time fixing my seat and came sixth. But because I'd won the first three races, I was invited to selection camp a few days later. At this camp, rowers are tried in different boats and in various combinations to see how they work with others.

I made the women's quad and was thrilled. After watching the 1976 Olympics, I had decided I wanted to compete internationally for Canada. From that moment on, there was no question in my mind that I would accomplish my goal (I like to think of it as determination rather than obsession). I had tried running, but didn't get the results I wanted. When I joined the women's rowing team, it was the proverbial dream-come-true for me.

As a rower, I was inexperienced and a technical disaster that spring. But the coaching staff were willing to take a chance on me as someone with potential. I must have been remarkably frustrating for the other people in the quad, because they were so much better than I was.

Not all rowers take the same route to international competition. Marnie McBean, who won two gold medals in Barcelona for team events, and a silver in women's singles at the '93 World Championships, began on the Junior team in 1986, then went to Senior B, and since '89 has been a member of the Senior A team. "I made the Junior team based on strength alone," McBean says. "But as I continued to row at the club and into the senior level, I worked to improve my technical side."

*Canadian women's eight at the U.S. Nationals in Indianapolis.*

National rowing has a three-tiered structure that is divided into different age groups, although rowers can be on the Senior A team at any age. The Junior team, for rowers aged eighteen and under, and the Senior B team, for athletes twenty-three and under, primarily give up-and-coming rowers an opportunity to work a bit more on their skills. These levels provide an intermediate step to the Senior A national team for those already successful at club rowing. International competitions are held for both Junior and Senior B rowers, but the Senior A team is the one that competes at the Olympics.

Once rowers reach this level, their training regimens become extremely demanding. In Canada, as a result of Mike Spracklen's influence, national team rowers train full-time in preparation for a major competition. Derek Porter, winner of gold in the men's eight at Barcelona and in men's singles at the '93 World Championships, says national team training differs mostly in volume from his previous training experiences. "With the eight, basically 7 A.M. to 5 P.M. was taken up either on the water or preparing to be on the water. We rowed for about ninety minutes three times a day and worked out with weights, as well," he explains. "I didn't do as much in the year leading up to the world championships, volume-wise. I was out in the boat twice a day, but I did more weights and indoor training. With the national team, training is intense—you're always training to race and you're shooting to be the best in the world."

The day-to-day training camp life of a national team athlete is almost completely focussed on rowing. Typically, they've finished their early morning workout and are ready to eat breakfast by about 10 A.M. An hour later they're back on the water, working on technique for another ninety minutes. Coaches follow the rowers in aluminum launches and suggest changes or different approaches: "Keep your blades well up on the return." Subtleties such as this can shave crucial seconds off the length of a race.

*Former national team coach Frank Read standing on the pier at Coal Harbour.*

*Former national team coach and Olympic medalist Dick McClure coaches at the Burnaby Lake Rowing Club, Burnaby, British Columbia.*

*Former national team coach Boris Klavora in the Delta Deas boathouse, Delta, British Columbia.*

*National team men's eight coxswain Terry Paul sleeping between workouts at the Elk Lake training facility.*

By one o'clock, everyone is ready for lunch. This is usually a quiet meal; no one has much energy for conversation, and the rowers and coaches feel the need to spend a few hours alone. After lunch, there's time for a short nap or a quick read, or sometimes a session in the weight room. Finally, it's time to climb back into the boats to track another 20 kilometres. Following the last workout, some of the rowers dive in for a swim, while others prepare for supper. This is the most relaxed part of the day: the workouts are finished and there is some free time before dinner and team meetings.

During dinner, the phone begins to ring, and rowers eagerly answer calls from spouses and partners, parents and siblings. Training is so stressful and exhausting that athletes relish these calls. The phone and the mail are their connections to loved ones and the world outside the camp. Those rowers who aren't on the phone, talk and joke together, or read quietly before bed. By 10:30 everyone is asleep, anticipating another day devoted to their sport.

The life of a national team rower involves a lower ratio of racing to training than regular club rowing. It breaks down to about ten percent racing and ninety percent training. And, as Derek Porter suggests, when you do race it's always in very high-pressure situations. National team rowers tend to pursue the sport as if it were a career, rather than something they simply love to do. They continue to enjoy rowing, but at the same time become more serious about it. As before, teammates are friends and supporters, but the barbecues and evening parties tend to disappear—no one has the time or energy to have an active social life.

Nor is it a life of luxuries. Canada has a funding system for national rowers in which athletes are "carded," or categorized as A, B, C, or D level, based on performance. An A card represents a stipend of $650 per month, and a D card, $350. It's not always quite enough to live on, but adequate for food and accommodation. Usually, athletes supplement this with a job, but given the intense training routine,

*The national team experiences midday collapse at Olympic gold-winning men's eight member Rob Marland's house, Brentwood College, Brentwood Bay, British Columbia.*

there's not much time for gainful employment. Consequently, most national team rowers live much like university students. Few of them own cars; most rely on bicycles. Frequently, they live in sparsely furnished basement suites, and the weekly grocery bill offers dilemmas such as whether to buy raisins or granola bars.

It's a simple way of life, according to Brenda Backer, who won bronze in women's doubles at the 1990 World Championships: "Everything's defined for you. You know exactly what you're going to be doing from day to day and there aren't many complications. Your short-term goals are all spelled out and within your reach. When you race, you get the results, that's it, and you're on to the next stage. I miss those days. There are so many choices to make in my life now. But when you're on the national team someone says, 'Okay, you're getting on that bus, going to that town; you're going to do this workout and eat this food.' It might seem awful to imagine someone controlling you that much, but when life becomes so simple, you have more appreciation for simple things, such as friendships. And the narrow focus makes it easier to get the job done."

This clearly defined purpose means athletes must also develop their goal-setting skills, something I firmly believe in. Working towards concrete goals benefits anyone, but is particularly necessary for national team rowers. As Cameron Harvey, winner of bronze in men's lightweight doubles at the 1986 World Championships, says, "You set a goal and you know exactly what the means are to achieve it. Say you want to win a medal in an international event. If you devote yourself entirely to it, there's a good chance you'll get the results you want. There are various means to reach that goal—training methods and techniques you can experiment with. The best way to succeed is to work hard

*An Argonaut Rowing Club crew rowing in the Head of the Charles Regatta outside Boston. The Head of Charles is the largest one-day regatta in the world.*

and work smartly. It's not a lot different than what goes on in the rest of life, but in athletics it's maybe easier to see."

Despite the rewards of national team life, it can also be a fairly tough existence. The rowers must move to a training centre, so they usually spend a lot of time away from their families and friends. To accommodate training and competition schedules, they become transient, learning to pack lightly and have few possessions. Often, because of the time and energy they must put into rowing, they compromise jobs, schooling and relationships—personal as well as social. And, of course, many athletes ultimately are *not* able to reach their goals in competition, although not all the non-winners are dissatisfied. Merely striving for something at that level—to be on the team means you are among the top rowers in the world—is an accomplishment. As Marnie McBean says, "Knowing I'm among the best, especially with the Canadian team, is a comforting thought when I'm on the starting line."

One of the things I enjoy most about rowing for the national team is the sense of mutual respect and support my colleagues give each other. Over the past ten years of training, I've never felt alone in achieving my goals; I've always had other athletes and coaches working hard alongside me. Rob Marland, who won gold in the men's eight at Barcelona, says he also gained a great deal from working in this environment. "In any group, each person brings different strengths," he says. "But on that crew, there was a particularly strong team feeling. For example, I needed to do a lot of work on squats [in the weight room]. Darren Barber would always help me, which indirectly helped the crew. Or, on days when we'd already put in a lot of hours, we might feel sore, or it would be raining and some of us might not want to go out again. But the enthusiasm of someone who did want to get back on the water would draw the group along."

*Men's national team prepares to lift their boat out of Elk Lake.*

Wendy Wiebe says she loves the people and the lifestyle of national team rowing: "It's unusual to find such a group of individuals who all like to work this hard. I'm thankful because I never would have met some of these people if not for rowing. And I've learned a lot about my own personality traits. I've developed a strong work ethic which I know I can apply to anything else and be successful."

Besides the athletes, coaches are a major component of the national team community. Many of them, like Brian Richardson, made the switch from competitive rowing to coaching, not always an easy transition. "For me it took a while to really become confident with coaching," Richardson says. "I'd rowed for Australia in two Olympics—in '76 and '80—and discovered it was hard to suddenly find myself on the bank instead of in the boat. Now I get a thrill from helping athletes reach their potential. I find it frustrating to work with beginners, but enjoy working with senior rowers to find some point of technique which gives them the extra few seconds advantage they need to be the best.

"In order to achieve excellence in anything—sport, business or whatever—you have to have dedication and single-mindedness. In some ways, by being on the national team, my private life may have suffered. I usually have to leave parties early, for example. And financially, perhaps I'm not as well off as I'd be if I'd put the same energy into another career or even certain other sports. But I don't feel I've missed out on anything. I've had a huge amount of joy and been all around the world with a lot of wonderful people because of rowing. So I never look back."

Certainly, the performance of our national team has been remarkable in the last few years. However, the Canadian rowing team wasn't always at the top in international competition. Mel Laforme, who rowed for Canada

*John Wallace strokes the national team men's eight in training.*

in four Olympic games (1976–88) remembers a time when things were different: "In my early days we were a miserably poor team. We were so far behind in so many ways—our training, our technique, our equipment, how we prepared for regattas. We did everything on a shoe-string budget, and every time we went to an international competition, there'd be a new manager. We would always be running out of money and end up taking the bus or renting bicycles to get to the course. Now I understand why we had so much trouble—when you start compromising all the little things, and you aren't committed to only the best, you just get further and further behind."

Fortunately, those days are over. Since the mid-80s, national team rowing in Canada has proved to be a successful effort. In Barcelona our team took four gold medals and one bronze; at the '93 World Championships, four golds, two silvers and a bronze. Obviously, the attitude and the approach have changed considerably.

Richardson feels that part of the Canadian team's recent achievement is attributable to its managerial system. "I have no doubt our program is much healthier than, for example, the Australian one," he says. "Canada has a strong national team concept in terms of a head coach—one person calling the shots and developing a program. The job I have here doesn't exist in Australian rowing. And the system here isn't hampered by politicking, infighting and rivalries. Another reason Canada has done so well the past few years is Doug Hamilton."

Hamilton, the vice-president of high performance for Rowing Canada, rowed with Mel Laforme in the national team quad between 1976 and 1988. He now helps create the vision of where the sport is going in this country. "Doug appoints people to various positions, and lets

*Jessica Monroe, double gold winner in the 1992 Olympic Women's Four and Eight, training on Elk Lake.*

*A Canadian women's team put their boat into the water during the U.S. Nationals at Indianapolis.*

*Men's national team training at Elk Lake.*

them get on with the work," Richardson says. "He's a very good devil's advocate for me. If I bring him a plan, he'll pull it to pieces. If it's still together by the end of our conversation, I know it must be good."

Of course, Richardson also acknowledges that much of the credit for the Canadian team's accomplishments must go to the athletes themselves: "To make it to the national team takes a strong mental approach and a will to work and develop yourself, apart from having a certain talent. The top athletes here are very strong mentally.

"On the physical side, rowing is very much a strength endurance event. Similarly, athletes must also be prepared to stick out the sport for the long term, setting at least three- or four-year goals. And they need to balance their lives out; they can't simply be dedicated to rowing. Those long-term goals must include private lives and careers. For example, I told the national team people they don't need to come to Victoria this year to train. They should get more study under their belts and row in their home areas. This way, it'll be easier when I ask them in '95 to come here full-time. I often give a lecture about what I call the 'raft of life.' I say that the raft has three pontoons: sport, private life and career. If one of those gets too far out of whack, the raft tips over."

*St. Catharines lightweight men approaching the Harvard boathouse during the Head of the Charles Regatta outside Boston.*

National team rowing holds many rewards, and a lifestyle that has its own appeal (although it may not suit everyone). The rewards cannot be measured in dollar signs, but in a deep feeling of satisfaction with goals achieved through hard work and tenacity. These days, the Canadian team seems to have a great many strengths, from the athletes to the coaches, on up to the management level. We're all pursuing this thing we don't expect will produce great fortunes; the only recognition we want is within the sport itself. Canada has spent a long time balancing the strengths of its national team, and it looks like we're heading straight down the course.

*Rowing encompasses a lot of the basic philosophies of life. It teaches you discipline, how to be the best at something, and that it's not so much what you're good at, it's the process. Now, if there's something I'm pretty sure I can accomplish, I just take the confidence I have from my rowing experiences and apply it to whatever I'm doing.*
—Brenda Backer, winner of bronze in the 1990 World Championships

# HISTORY

## INTRODUCTION

It is morning and the sun has barely risen above the trees. No sound disturbs the tranquillity of a scene still drowsy with sleep. Calm waters reflect trees, mountains and gossamer mists. Suddenly, a slim, highly polished craft appears out of the mists, its crew straining on their oars. The oars enter the water, creating seething grey-green pools, propelling the hull smoothly through the otherwise unruffled waters. Swiftly but silently the shell glides towards an unseen destination. After the shell's passage, the water returns to its former peace. In spite of all the force and power, it is as if no vessel had ever passed this way.

This early-morning summer scene is repeated daily across Canada, sometimes on a lake that nestles at the foot of mountains, sometimes on a river that passes through farmland or even through the centre of a city. It is a scene that takes place in summer and even in winter and one that has been repeated almost unchanged for over a hundred years.

Men and (since the 1970s in Canada) women, sit facing the stern and propel their craft forward by means of sweeping the oars through the water in a co-ordinated application of force. The movement of oars and bodies in unison creates a graceful, flowing sequence. This grace, together with the power of the strokes and the smooth but swift glide of the shell, epitomizes the aesthetics of the sport.

Rowing, according to Baron Pierre de Coubertin, founder of the modern Olympic games, is that most beautiful of sports.

## EARLY HISTORY

The basic practice of the sport has remained the same since Virgil first described a boat race two thousand years ago, but some things, such as the boat, have changed with time. The early boats were rough craft, made wide of beam to ensure sturdiness and to allow as much leverage of the oar as possible. Today's boats are slim and gleam with the finish of modern plastics; leverage is gained by the use of "outriggers" that move the swing point of the oar out over the water some 20 or 30 centimetres outside the hull.[1] The hull's smoothness and light weight is often compared to an eggshell, and hence the modern craft are referred to as "shells."

The old heavy, carvel-built boats[2] were rowed usually by four or six oarsmen who sat on fixed seats and used a short, choppy stroke. This style of rowing was dictated by the length of the oarsman's body and arms, and by the construction of the boat. In contrast, today's oarsmen row with the benefit of a sliding seat, which allows full use of the legs, and because there is little advantage to swinging the body in order to get greater length, the resulting style is long, controlled and smooth. This very smooth control enhances the aesthetic effect of the oarsman's efforts.

Early races were rowed over a mile or two and included a U-turn. Thus races started and finished at the same point. It is still so practised at the annual regatta held since 1816 on Quidi Vidi Lake in the centre of St. John's, Newfoundland. Elsewhere, however, most rowing today is conducted over a straight distance of

2,000 metres. Spectators can either sit in a grandstand and watch the last quarter of the race or follow the race for its entire length in a boat or, more commonly, on television. Races last about six minutes.

The crews of early boats would not match the picture of beauty and grace conjured up by modern athletes. Many of these early oarsmen were professional boatmen, usually fishermen, to whom the sun, rough salt seas and strong winds were familiar, and whose hard physiques and faces reflected their continuing battles with the elements. When they raced, they raced for material gain, and when they were not racing they followed their trade upon the waters and trained incidentally as they fished.

Rowing, a vital element in early European transportation, has provided opportunities for racing for thousands of years. In his *Aeneid*, written between 30 and 19 B.C., Virgil described such a race, in which one of the contestants comes to grief in approaching too closely to the offshore rock that marked the turning point. Not until 1726, however, did rowing races begin to take on a sense of structure and permanence. In that year, Thomas Doggett, an actor in London, England, established an annual race for young apprentices on the River Thames in England, and this event still takes place today.

It is ironic that rowing had to be imported into Canada, land of lakes and rivers. The indigenous craft was the canoe, fashioned out of wood and bark by the original inhabitants. Indeed, as a means of transportation, the canoe offered many advantages: it was light enough to be carried over portages, and its crew faced forward and could thus take avoiding action when threatened by dangers such as rapids. But the canoe had two disadvantages: it was less stable and it could carry much less than the wider and sturdier boats propelled by oars. On the still waters of the large rivers and in the rougher offshore seas, the rowing boat offered increased safety and a more economic passage for freight.

Once the rowboat arrived, the development of rowing as a sport quickly followed, though it remained for some time the preserve of fishermen and, occasionally, visiting military. The earliest rowing race in Canada was held in Halifax Harbour in 1811 between the garrison and a visiting Royal Navy warship. That race, the Royal Navy won.

From the 1820s on, rowing spread westward across the country and regattas quickly became a feature of festivals in those towns and villages where a suitable stretch of water could be found. Some regattas went on to become annual events, of which a few still continue. A Toronto regatta, first held around 1840, was the forerunner of an annual event that has continued in one form or another until the present day. On July 1, oarsmen, oarswomen and canoeists bring their shells to the Long Pond on Toronto Island for a full day's racing. Set in the island's carefully tended parks and gardens, it is an ideal place for the citizens of Toronto and surrounding areas to enjoy watching the sport in all its glory.

By the mid-1830s rowing had established itself firmly in Ontario. The rivers on or near the St. Lawrence were ideally suited for the sport. Many had long stretches of water sheltered by high banks covered with thick woods, which provided both a measure of protection against the wind and a vantage point from which spectators could cheer their favourite teams. The attraction of taking a picnic to a grassy hill overlooking water has endured to this day. A rowing race gave an added thrill to the bucolic pleasures of such an outing.

In almost all urban areas, rowing races were held just outside the city limits, where the sylvan settings provided a means for the inhabitants to get away from the urban grime and grind. Even if nature could not supply a respite from the dreariness of work, the festivities surrounding a regatta usually could. Fun fairs and refreshment tents were set up on the grounds bordering the race course and, if a little further excitement was sought, there were ample opportunities for wagering—even enormous sums—on the outcome of the races.

This early Canadian interest in the sport was not confined to competitions at home. Reports of regattas held outside the country were read avidly, and when a Canadian crew came away as the victors, as happened occasionally, the national pride, if not the private purse, grew enormously, particularly if the losers were American.

In 1855 an eight-oared boat from Saint John, New Brunswick, manned by the "Superior" crew, beat a champion American crew at Boston, Massachusetts, and brought home a handsome prize of $2,000 for their efforts. In 1858 the Toronto Shakespeare Club challenged a boastful Metropolitan Club of Chicago to a race over 5 miles for a prize of $5,000. The crew included a young Richard Tinning as cox. When the Americans objected that Tinning was too light, the Torontonians pressed a bystander to join them and pulled the two coxswains over the course. By winning despite the added weight, the Canadians clearly established their superiority.

## The Paris Four

The real strength of early Canadian rowing was developed on the rough waters of the Bay of Fundy amid the fogs and storms of the Atlantic coast. There a crew developed who launched Canada's standing in rowing into the ranks of the world class.

In 1867 this crew left Saint John, New Brunswick, for Paris, France, to participate in the international regatta that was part of the World Exposition. The regatta took place as Canada was being proclaimed a confederacy under the British Crown, but this important political event was eclipsed in the media by the anticipation of the race.

A total of $6,000 was raised by the community and the provincial government as witness to the pride and confidence inspired by the crew. One reporter wrote: "Although to the great International Exposition we have sent no elaborate works of art, no specimen of ingenious handicraft, no sample of the products of mine or field, we have nevertheless sent to Paris such an 'exhibit' of our energy our hardihood and pluck as shall render up famous among all the famed at that grand international tournament." He was to be proved right.

The 1867 crew would hardly fit today's highly polished image of world-class amateur sportsmen. Today's star athletes are presented as educated individuals who personify the ideals of clean, graceful living. These men were described as rough, ill-bred and rude tobacco-chewing fishermen. But in spite of their appearance and perhaps their manners, they could row.

Samuel Hutton was the first member of what came to be called the Paris crew, and he rowed in the number-two seat. He was an Irishman who had come to Canada at an early age, around the time of the potato famines in his native country. At 5 feet 9 inches and 157 pounds, he was described as "well proportioned with prominent cheek bones and a pleasing countenance." Elijah Ross was a Nova Scotia lighthouse keeper who had moved to Saint John at an early age. At 5 feet 11 inches and 158 pounds, he would occupy the number-three seat in the boat. The two men met in 1862 and rowed together for two years, although without much success. In 1864 they introduced Robert Fulton into their crew. Fulton would eventually become stroke.[3] At 6 feet 1 inch and 165 pounds, he was well suited to the task. Described as "tough as nails," he set a demanding pace in the boat. George Price was the final member of the crew and was five years older than the others. He brought with him much-needed maturity and experience. The 5-foot-10-inch, 145-pound fisherman's sharp, curt, barking orders in the boat would annoy his crewmates, but he was good at what he did, and he had a fierce determination to win.[4]

The crew was not warmly received in Europe. The English coaches and reporters scoffed at these colonials. Not only was their equipment not in the latest style of light, smooth, polished hulls, but they did not even possess respectable racing uniforms in the colours of their club or country, as was considered necessary for a crew to win. They presented a curious spectacle: The correspondent the *Manchester Guardian* pointed out that "among the strange looking people whom this regatta has brought together, not the least strange were the four sturdy New Brunswickers.... With their flesh-coloured jerseys, dark cloth trousers, leather braces and bright pink caps, they were in strik-

*The Paris Four: Canada's first winners of a World Championship, by winning in 1867 the Fours events at the Paris World Exhibition.*—NAC C14065

ing contrast to their neat competitors." Clearly, lacking the appropriate equipment and not dressed properly for the occasion, this entry was of no consequence. England, dominator of the Empire and dominant in sport, could concentrate on more worthy opponents.

Two races were held, one for in-rigged boats and one for out-rigged boats, with six entries for each race. The first race was with a turn, while the second was a straightaway.

In the first race, the Saint John boat took the lead by a length and a quarter to the turn. On the way back, the French crew from Paris made a determined effort to catch up, but a short, quick burst from the Canadians quashed their ambitions. The New Brunswickers passed the grandstand with their "stroke cooly waving his hat at the crowd, rowing with one hand and winning easily."

Six boats started in the second race: Paris, London, Saint John, Boulonge, Hamburg and Oxford University. The Canadian boat at 200 pounds weighed 6 pounds more than any of the rival boats. Taking an early lead, rowing forty-six to forty-seven strokes per minute, the New Brunswickers finished first, "talking and laughing in the easiest manner possible." The Canadian Paris crew had won so handily that the same *Manchester Guardian* correspondent noted that "it should make English oarsmen and English boatbuilders reconsider the first principles of their art."

The win over England was especially sweet for the then still colonial Dominion, and the crew returned in triumph to a tumultuous welcome by several thousand citizens. The city of Saint John gave them a parade, a cash prize of $500, a reception, and the "freedom of the city."[5]

With fame came challengers, but the crew remained unbeaten until 1870, when a boat from Newcastle on Tyne managed to win at Lachine by a single yard. The first defeat of the Paris crew set the scene for one of the most poignant events in Canadian rowing history.

The Great Race, as it came to be called, was held on the Kennebecasis River as a grudge match designed to expunge the defeat of Lachine and bring back the pride that a community held in its sportsmen. Of the original Tyne crew, only the stroke, James Renforth, was present. The race was over 6 miles, and the prize was a purse of five hundred pounds sterling and the championship. The event was so hyped by the press that over twenty-five thousand people flocked to the city from Eastern Canada and the Northeast United States.

For the first 200 yards, rowing at over forty strokes a minute, the two crews raced neck and neck, and then Renforth dropped the rate to thirty-nine. Fulton kept his pace at forty-one and began to take the lead so that by the half-mile mark, there was open water between the two boats. Fearing that they were losing contact, the Tyne crew put on a burst, which made up the distance, but the Paris crew put on their own burst and opened the gap again. At the three-quarter mark, the Tyne captain called for another burst when Renforth dropped his oar and fell back into the arms of his crewmates. The boat stopped and was rowed to shore. Renforth was taken back to his quarters, and died there at 8:48 A.M., half an hour after the Paris crew, unaware of the tragic events, completed the race, to the rapturous cheers of the watching multitudes.

The Great Race marked—with the exception of the win by the Smith Nickerson crew of Halifax at the Philadelphia Centennial Regatta of 1876—the end of the era of the professional racing crews for Canadian rowing, and today only the village of Renforth in New Brunswick commemorates what was the sporting event of the decade. The next era was to be the golden age of Canadian sculling.

## The Scullers

Sculling is the art of moving a boat by using two oars, one in each hand. Usually, there is only one person in the boat; hence the class name: the single. In Canada, sculling started as an annual competitive event in 1858 when Dr. Charles Cogswell donated a silver belt and the interest from one hundred pounds sterling to be presented to the winner of the Halifax Harbour Championship. From 1860 to 1864 the event was won by George Lovett, but in 1865, it was won by George Brown, who is considered to have been, at least potentially, the greatest Canadian sculler in the middle of the nineteenth century.

Born in 1839 in the small Nova Scotia community of Herring Cove, Brown was a fisherman by trade. He won permanent pos-

session of two Cogswell belts by twice winning, five times in succession, the Harbour Championship. In 1871 Brown challenged Joseph Sadler of England for the World Sculling Championship, and though the race went to Sadler, Brown was accorded a moral victory on the basis of two factors: Sadler was accused of using unfair tactics and he refused ever to meet Brown in competition again. Brown went on to win and successfully defend the American Sculling Championship, but his promising career was cut short in the winter of 1873 when he died at Halifax General Hospital.

In 1868, while Brown was excelling in Nova Scotia, Dick Tinning of the Toronto Rowing Club (and of the Shakespeare Club's two coxswains fame) introduced the first single built along modern lines and won the Junior Toronto Bay Championship. The slim craft, called the Cigarette because of its shape, gave Tinning an edge over his opponents.[6] Under rowing conditions comparable to today's, he was able to win the Senior Championship of Toronto Bay in 1869, and the Canadian Championship the year after that. It was the beginning of a period of dramatic successes, when Canadian scullers dominated American and even world competition.

In the two decades that followed Tinning's success, Canadian scullers were phenomenally successful in winning and defending Canadian, American, English and even World Championship titles. Because Tinning was the first to introduce the modern single shell and was the first of these successful Canadian scullers, he is often regarded as the father of present-day rowing in Canada.

Almost a dozen Canadians vied for the available championships in the second half of the nineteenth century. In a bewildering round of challenges, they competed against each other, and titles rotated rapidly and fairly regularly among them. Names such as Warren Smith, Albert Hamm, Patrick Conley and John McKay of the Maritimes, and J. Scholes, Tommy Louden, William McCann and J. Douglas were as familiar to the people of the day as the names of hockey and baseball stars are today.

*George Brown 1839–1875, champion oarsman.*
—Collection of Nova Scotia Sport Heritage

These sculling greats and their promoters were a colourful group of people. Boastful to the point of arrogance, they inspired followers the professionals of today can only envy. Bets on their abilities, won and lost, were even by today's measures exorbitant: $5,000 was not an unusual wager—a staggering amount in its modern equivalent. Their racing tactics included dirty tricks that in modern times would not find much favour, but they also inspired an enduring admiration. Competitors sometimes found their equipment smashed, or their rivals would try to win by using shortcuts, thus failing to complete the course; but on the other hand, their pursuit of excellence based on physical and technical training is still the approach followed by today's top-class athletes.

Robert "Bob" Berry of Toronto was the first black Canadian to scull successfully. A man of imposing stature and great courage, Berry was awarded a silver medal in 1868 for the heroic rescue of a crew whose ship went aground off Toronto in a severe winter storm. He was a sculler who regularly competed and often won in the regattas held in Ontario. But he was also human and easily fell victim his opponents' tactics. In a race with J. Scholes, Berry was so drawn into an argument that he was still stuttering and mumbling to himself twenty seconds after the starter's gun went off; nor did he manage to make up the tremendous handicap.

Race tactics were also carefully planned to include activities before the race. Tinning won against Berry by inviting him to practise starts before the race. Berry obliged, thinking that one or two in the morning would accommodate this reasonable request. Tinning, however, persuaded Berry to practise all morning under the blazing sun, and by race time Berry was as limp as a rag.

Tommy Louden similarly meticulously planned the defeat of a bragging Englishman named Kempster. Louden was best at a 2-mile distance, while Kempster reportedly was good over short distances, so Louden insisted on a 5-mile race, which he won

*George Lovett, one of the most respected oarsmen of the 1860s, won the Halifax Harbour Championships in 1859, 1861, 1862 and 1863, losing to his chief rival, George Brown, in 1864.*

—Photograph collection, Public Archives of Nova Scotia

*After winning the Philadephia regatta in 1876, Ned Hanlan was considered to be Canada's foremost sculler, an honour challenged by the champion of the Maritimes, Wallace Ross. When the two scullers actually did meet, Ross was humiliated and Hanlan went on to win the World Championship.*

—NAC C66120

easily. In the subsequent rerow, Kempster was rammed by a spectator and, believing it had been deliberate, next appeared with a pistol neatly tucked into his boat, in full view. The precaution proved unnecessary, but Kempster still lost.

During 1874 and 1875 Alex Brayley dominated the St. John's harbour scene. At 5 feet 8 inches and 160 pounds, he was a superb athlete. After winning the Halifax Harbour Championship in 1875, he next travelled to Philadelphia for the 1876 Centennial Regatta, together with the Paris crew. The event, which attracted the best scullers and oarsmen of the day, proved to be a momentous occasion.

The Paris crew, which had been actively training for a couple of years, was defeated by the Smith Nickerson crew of Halifax in a sadly anticlimactic last race. But the singles race made up for the disappointment.

Brayley reached the finals, but there met for the first time a twenty-one-year-old sculler from Toronto, Ned Hanlan.

## Ned Hanlan and Wallace Ross

Ned Hanlan was the son of Irish immigrants. In the face of opportunities limited by the working class from which they came, the Hanlans chose to make their living on the waters of Lake Ontario. Though the family started out in this country as fishing folk, they eventually prospered enough to purchase a hotel. This establishment, a meeting place for many of the residents of Toronto Island, was where young Ned was born on July 12, 1855.

Rowing quickly became part of young Ned's life; indeed, he rowed every time he left the island, and by the time he was sixteen he was ready to enter but not to win his first competition against, among other competitors, Bob Berry. It was the start of a long career that would bring him into competition with Luther Plaisted, the American champion, and Alex Brayley in Philadelphia at the Centennial Regatta of 1876. Brayley was Maritimes champion and the Canadian favoured to win.

By the start of the final race, Hanlan had already galvanized the American crowd by easily defeating Plaisted in the semifinal. In one of the most exciting races ever witnessed at the Centennial Regatta, Brayley was beaten by the newcomer,

Hanlan, despite his best efforts. While the victorious Hanlan returned to Toronto a hero with a $1,500 prize, Brayley collected $400 and went home to face the prospect of a race there with Wallace Ross.

Wallace Ross was Saint John's contribution to what has been called the golden age of sculling. A strapping fellow 6 feet tall, Ross first attracted notice when he beat Robert Fulton in 1873. He went on to achieve several wins in the Maritimes, including victories over Alex Brayley. Flushed with success, Ross had challenged Hanlan, and when the latter failed to respond, he had brashly claimed to be the champion of Canada. After Philadelphia, promoters felt that a Ross–Brayley rematch was in order.

Because he had already beaten Brayley twice that year, Ross awaited the upcoming race with eager anticipation. When he won by a full minute and a half, the local supporters believed Ross's boast about being champion of Canada and were convinced they had the fastest man in North America, if not the world.

Ross went on to several victories and again challenged Hanlan. When Hanlan again refused to rise to the challenge, Ross sublimely proclaimed himself the fastest man in Canada.

Hanlan was biding his time, training in Toronto Harbour. He was perfecting his mastery over a new development in rowing equipment. Hitherto, oarsmen had rowed sitting on a fixed seat. But now, the first sliding seats appeared and allowed the oarsman to use his legs and so achieve a smoother and more powerful drive. This feature, more than any other, transformed rowing from the style that had been in practice for centuries into the style used today. The results achieved by the adoption of this new way of rowing were significant improvements, not only in the power the oarsman could apply, but in the swifter passage of the boat through the water. Times over distances started to drop dramatically.[7]

Hanlan was not the first to use the sliding seat, but he was the first to master it, and Ross was the first prominent sculler to suffer defeat when he failed to follow this style. In the end, when Ross and Hanlan finally met for the Canadian Championship, Ross returned to Saint John devastated by the ease with which he had been beaten.

Ross went into a decline until 1880. He started the year on an unfortunate note. In a race on the Charles River, in Boston,

Ross's opposition, a man named "Frenchy" Johnson started before the signal to start had been given. The referee refused to call Johnson back and Ross refused to row after him. When the race was awarded to Johnson, the crowd turned ugly and the referee called off all bets. When, later that evening, Ross came across Johnson in a tavern, the police had to be called in to sort out the incident.

In June of that year Ross entered a race sponsored by the makers of a popular stomach remedy, the Hop Bitters Company. Hanlan and Plaisted led from the beginning of the race, setting a tremendous pace in order to be the first around the turning buoy. The effort exhausted both men, whereupon Ross caught up and, overtaking first one and then the other, set such a pace that none of the competitors, including Hanlan, were able to keep up. Ross was first across the line and unexpectedly won the big race.

The success rekindled an interest in his career, and he travelled to England, where he beat Ed Trickett, the Australian who had just lost the World Championship title to Hanlan. For the next three years Canada could claim in Ross and Hanlan the world's best scullers.

In 1881 Toronto hosted a grand international regatta that attracted the greatest scullers of the age. The two top Canadians were joined by Teemer, Hosmer, Courtenay, and Ten Eyck of the United States, and Trickett. Here, also, a young Canadian by the name of Jake Gaudaur made his appearance. Gaudaur would one day join the ranks of the champions, but not this time. On September 21, 1881, Ross reached the pinnacle of his career when he won the Toronto regatta. Having beaten Hanlan and Trickett, he could justifiably claim to be the unofficial world champion.

Ross challenged Hanlan again, and again Hanlan refused, to which a furious Ross boasted that Hanlan had little to offer. It was enough, and Hanlan finally accepted. In 1883, in Ogdensburg, New York, Hanlan made Ross eat his words. Over a 4-mile course and to the surprise of almost everyone, Hanlan humiliated Ross, winning by over a minute. Hanlan was again undisputed world champion.

Ross retired four years later and went to England, where he established a reputation as a swordsman. His departure left the field clear for Hanlan.

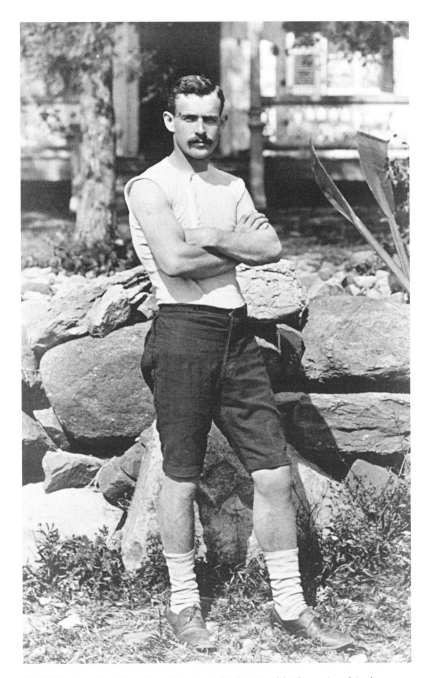

*Ned Hanlan, the first Canadian to hold the World Championship for sculling.*—NAC C25318

118

## Ned Hanlan Alone

When, in 1874, Hanlan won the Ontario Championship, he attracted the attention of backers who formed the Hanlan Club, providing the means for the young oarsman to fully devote his time to rowing.

The support he received was amply justified at the 1876 Centennial Regatta in Philadelphia. He took an early lead over his competitors, and established what was to become a trademark of his racing technique: he stopped to see where the others had rowed to and to look at the large crowd. Even with such stops, and just when it seemed as if someone else would take the lead, Hanlan sculled away, leaving the increasingly frustrated competitors never to catch up. As Brayley passed Hanlan in the opposite direction, heading for the turn, Hanlan waved to the crowd. For Brayley that was the final insult. Disheartened, he finished some three lengths behind Hanlan—or, as he was known from his racing colours, the Boy in Blue. In the final, Hanlan not only won, but set a new course record of 21 minutes 9.5 seconds over 5 kilometres.

In 1878, one year after beating Ross for the Canadian Championship, Hanlan won the American Championship by beating "Eph" Morris. In 1879 he went to England, where his arrival caused more curiosity than interest. But that curiosity changed to intense interest when he won the English Championship by eleven lengths after rowing the course fifty-five seconds faster than anyone else ever had.

Hanlan was clearly made of the superior material of champions, but the same could not be said of the manner in which championships were conducted, as was demonstrated by his experiences against a young American sculler by the name of Charles Courtney. They first met at Lachine, Quebec, where Hanlan was able to win by the slimmest margin of his career, just over a length. As far as the newspapers were concerned, the race was not over and the rematch was organized for Mayville, New York, and sponsored by the Hop Bitters Manufacturing Company.

When Hanlan launched his boat at the start of that race, it broke in two and the race was postponed for a week. On the day of the second start, Courtney announced that his boat had been sawn in half. The referee ruled that the race would start nonethe-

OFFICIAL PROGRAMME.

# DOMINION DAY CELEBRATION,
*Brockville, Ont., July 1, 1878.*

SCULLING RACE, for $1,000—$500 to First; $300 to Second; $200 to Third.

| | Time Starting. | Time Returning. |
|---|---|---|
| EDWARD HANLAN, Toronto, CHAMPION OF AMERICA, Winner of the Celebrated International Match, at Pittsburg, June 20th, 1878. Color, Red Cap and Blue Shirt. | | |
| A. ELLIOTT, Toronto, Ont. Color, Yellow Cap. | | |
| FRED A. PLAISTED, Boston, Mass. Color, Cardinal and Gray Shirt. | | |
| JOHN KENNEDY, Boston, Mass. Color, White Cap, Cardinal and Gray Shirt. | | |
| JAMES A. TENEYCK, Peekskill, N.Y. Color, Blue Cap. | | |
| PAT LUTHER, Pittsburgh, Pa. Color, Green Cap. | | |
| WM. McKEN, Toronto, Ont. Color, Flesh-colored Shirt and Blue Pants. | | |
| JAS. H. RILEY, Saratoga. White Cap, White Shirt, Blue Pants. | | |

The Contestants will start at a point opposite the Custom House Wharf, turn separate Stake Boats, two miles down the River, and return to starting point.
All steamboats and skiffs are Prohibited crossing the course at any time during the Race.
The start will be made at 5 p.m., if the water is favorable.

—Courtesy Doug Marshall, Brockville Rowing Club

less and that Courtney must row in another boat. But once the race started, Hanlan rowed alone and discovered, on getting back to the boathouse, that both Courtney and the sponsor had disappeared with the prize money.

The rematch was eventually set for Washington, on May 19, 1878. It was to be called "the most contemptible failure in American boating history." Courtney quickly lost the lead and began rowing erratically. At the 3-kilometre mark, well before the official turn, he turned and rowed towards the finish line. Hanlan, seeing that Courtney was not about to row over the full course, increased his rating and still managed to win. One further win, this time against the American James Riley, and Hanlan was undisputed Canadian and United States champion. The next target was the world title.

The November 15, 1880, race for the World Championship on the River Thames in London, England, between Hanlan and the Australian Ed Trickett, was a meeting of contrasts. Their countries lay at opposite ends of the world, and their physical appearances were equally different: Hanlan was small and lightweight, Trickett was well over 6 feet and 200 pounds. It was an event that generated enormous excitement and betting. Over $100,000 was wagered in Australia alone, and two days before the race, a $42,000 bet was wired from Toronto. In those days,

—Courtesy Doug Marshall, Brockville Rowing Club

$1,500 was the annual salary of the president of a mid-size company, so that bets totalling $100,000 then would be equivalent to bets of between $10 million and $20 million today.

Trickett expected to maintain his title with ease, yet the papers of the day reported a certain tautness about him that suggested he had nagging doubts about this young upstart from Canada. If there were any such doubts, they were well founded. Hanlan's gamesmanship almost exceeded his rowing ability, because by one third of the way into the race, he had opened up a three-boat lead. Then he stopped rowing, and Trickett, encouraged by seeing him stop, attempted to close the gap. No sooner did he begin to try, than Hanlan started up again and quickly retrieved his original lead. It happened again at the halfway mark, again when Hanlan spotted William Elliott, whom he had beaten for the English Championship, again as he passed the Canadian headquarters, and again with half a kilometre to go. Suddenly, a ray of hope for the fading Trickett: it appeared that all was not lost, because Hanlan suddenly slumped over his oars and drifted on the course. Trickett pulled even, sensing victory, but just as he was about to pass, Hanlan flashed a smile and took off, this time zigzagging down the course as he began rowing, using one oar then the other. Hanlan won easily, and Trickett retired quietly and refused to see anyone.

In the rematch, Hanlan won by almost a minute and a half, turned and rowed back up the course until he met Trickett, then turned and managed to beat the Australian again.

From 1880 to 1884 Hanlan maintained almost total control of world sculling, losing only to Ross in Toronto in 1881. He travelled extensively until August 16, 1884, when he met William Beach on the Paramatta River in Australia and was defeated for the world title. It was the end of a ten-year reign, even though Hanlan tried again to win in 1885 and 1887. Canada was not to have a world champion again until 1896, when Jake Gaudaur would bring the coveted title back home.

## Jake Gaudaur

Jacob Gaudaur was born on April 4, 1858, in a place near Orillia, Ontario, that later became the village of Atherley. Early on in life, he displayed a strong competitive streak, and frequently enjoyed canoe racing with the Ojibwa on the nearby Rama Reservation or racing in skiffs with his friends at the Narrows. Lakes Couchiching and Simcoe provided the training grounds for Jake's career in the field of professional sculling.

His first chance for competition came in 1876, when he was persuaded to enter a rowboat race on Lake Couchiching. Despite doubts about his ability to beat older and more experienced men, Gaudaur had an easy victory. It was all the impetus he needed to begin grooming himself for future competitions.

Over the next four years Gaudaur rowed almost entirely on Canadian waters, competing both in singles and in doubles with his brother Frank. There were several opportunities for competition, both in Orillia and in neighbouring Barrie, especially on festival days such as Victoria and Dominion Day and on the Civic holiday in August. It was a sign of the popularity of the sport that rowing went on as late as possible in the year; indeed, one event was reported as requiring the spectators to drive back to town in sleighs after the races were over, and young boys skated over the course next day.

Gaudaur's races were sometimes controversial, and sometimes the controversy could last several years. In 1936 a seventy-nine-year-old Tom Foley of Collingwood challenged Gaudaur to a rematch of a race held in 1881. The dispute centred on a golden oar trophy emblematic of the district rowing championship. Whoever won it twice could take permanent possession of it. By 1881 both Foley and Gaudaur had won it once, and when Gaudaur won, he took it home. Foley wanted an opportunity to win it back, since he felt that his 1881 performance had not reflected his real skill. Foley did not dispute Gaudaur's victory, only his own "new-fangled, patented, gadgety sliding seat arrangement," which had failed to operate properly. The seventy-eight-year-old Gaudaur's response was, "I beat Foley fifty-five years ago and I can beat him now; I am not afraid to race anyone my own age.... Nobody is going to dare me when it comes to rowing." The race never took place.

*Jake Gaudaur, world champion 1896–1901*—NAC C55224

In 1882 Gaudaur went to the United States, to St. Louis, Missouri, and established himself as a first-rate sculler by competing in and winning every match except two, and in these two he took third. In 1886, with a growing reputation, Gaudaur challenged for the Single Sculling Championship of America, "champion" being a title which had so far eluded him. On June 12, in Pullman, Illinois, he achieved a decisive one-quarter-mile victory and became the singles sculling champion of America. It was clear that he revelled in his new role, because in a rematch on July 2 in Winnipeg, "he indulged in the old Hanlan trick of taking off his hat and waving it to the spectators."

Gaudaur next challenged William Beach for the World Championship, which Beach had taken from Hanlan two years earlier. The race was arranged for London, England.

Though Gaudaur had won the American Championship, the forthcoming race against Beach did not generate much excitement. Gaudaur himself was not prone to making colourful public statements or rash promises, and there was probably little faith that he was ready to bring home a World Championship. Gaudaur was heard to say modestly, "I believe I have a fair chance." Beach won, but it was reported that Jake had given "the Australian the hardest push that he ever received," a view that Beach himself afterwards confirmed. Although Jake expressed the wish for another chance, he did not have the opportunity to travel to the Australian's homeland before Beach retired, unbeaten, in 1888. Nonetheless, thirty-five years later, Jake fondly recalled his contest with Beach on the Thames as the hardest race he ever rowed.

Gaudaur lost his American Championship title in 1887 and endured a three-year slump in his career. By 1890 he began to recover, and by 1896 he had conquered all of his North American rivals as well as several English opponents. Although unofficially proclaimed by his North American public as the world champion, he refused to accept the title without a race. In the summer of 1896 the opportunity to meet the reigning world champion, James Stanbury of Australia, presented itself. In response to repeated challenges, Stanbury announced that he would be ready to meet the Canadian in September in England. Since this was the only event of significance in which Gaudaur had not yet distinguished himself, Gaudaur, at thirty-eight years of age, accepted with alacrity.

The race took place over the same course where Gaudaur had been beaten by William Beach some ten years earlier. Back at home, Hanlan expressed the opinion that the Australian would have no difficulty in beating Gaudaur. It was a view generally shared, since Stanbury was ten years the younger.

The prophecies of doom were proved unfounded on September 7, when Gaudaur finished the $4^1/_4$ course some 200 yards ahead of Stanbury. It was reported that, while the first half of the race had been a "pretty struggle," Jake had literally paddled the course for the last half, leaving Stanbury many lengths behind.

His homecoming was a triumph. He was welcomed by many thousand well-wishers and escorted from the waterfront to Queen's Park, Toronto, by an elaborate procession of cars, bicycles and marching bands. There was a welcome from the mayor, a purse of $900 donated by admirers, a handshake from Hanlan and, best of all, the news that his second wife, Ida, had given birth to their first child, a daughter.

Following his win, Gaudaur's professional rowing engagements were less frequent. During his five-year reign as the world champion, he entered only three major competitions. He successfully defended his North American title against Erastus Rogers of Massachusetts in 1897 and his world title against Bob Johnston of Vancouver in 1898.

In April 1901 another professional sculler wished to race Gaudaur for his title. George Towns of Australia responded to Gaudaur's challenge to the world that "he would meet all comers," and a match was arranged, a race to be held on September 4 on Lake of the Woods at Rat Portage, Ontario. The prize was a purse of $2,500 and the World Championship.

Gaudaur was reported as training twice a day by the end of July and "in splendid form." Towns arrived in Rat Portage in the first week of August and put in a great deal of training. By the end of August, both scullers were reported ready, although Gaudaur's backers were not quite so sure. There was some basis for their misgivings, for, although smaller, the Australian had been training and racing regularly over the past three years. Furthermore, the Australian was ten years younger. But Gaudaur was confident and, on the day before the match, expected to win. On race day, September 4, the odds were in Gaudaur's favour. Unfortunately, the weather proved uncooperative and the race was postponed for three days. When the race did start, Towns set off at a good clip, and half a mile from the start had a lead of a length and was rowing smoothly. Towns reduced his rate from thirty-three to twenty-eight but Gaudaur was still rowing thirty-two and unable to close the gap; indeed, Towns increased his lead. The result was never in doubt: an easy win for the Anglo-Australian by three lengths.

The loss of the championship was not greeted bitterly by Gaudaur's supporters. They recognized that he had sustained a lengthy, successful and honourable career, and these virtues were not forgotten in the aftermath of the defeat. But the end it was, because Gaudaur announced his retirement from athletic competition and thus signalled an effective end to professional rowing in Canada. The void would soon be filled by amateurs.

Amateurism in sport means the playing of a sport for the love of it. It had existed for centuries, rising to great heights in England during the middle of the nineteenth century and slowly spreading to other countries. By the 1870s, however, amateurism and professionalism in sport collided when the aim of winning for glory and renown began to find more favour than the aim of winning for material gain. In addition, the outcome of a professional race was no longer considered a measure of an athlete's abilities, but more often the result of the influence of the bettors. With large sums of money at stake, the attraction began to fade. Within the sport of rowing itself, the amateurs had become frustrated at the regularity with which people who earned their livelihood by rowing won trophies and prizes. At the turn of the century, motorboats were available to few and so fishermen, pilots, ferrymen and lighthouse keepers all rowed as part of their daily lives. In doing so they developed not only a proficiency in the techniques of rowing, but also the strength and stamina the sport demands. The amateurs, many of whom followed more sedentary lives as clerks and businessmen, found they did not have the time to develop similar competence, and so were regularly beaten in competition. In frustration, the amateurs retreated to the protection of clubs restricted to amateurs and, by excluding anyone who might row as part of their trade, competed among themselves. In this way the amateurs established a pattern for the sport in which R. Tait McKenzie would later find a true expression of the ideals of *aidos,* which he described as "clean, honest and manly sport, that makes the sting of defeat nothing when weighed against the consciousness of having won dishonourably or by subterfuge."

In 1880 clubs formed the Canadian Association of Amateur Oarsmen to co-ordinate and regulate the sport of amateur rowing, and loftily proclaimed the ideals of abstinence from drinking alcohol, smoking and gambling.

One of the first acts of the new association was the establishment of an annual regatta to be called the association's regatta. Based on the ideals of amateur sport, it was open only to athletes from the amateur clubs, was run in accordance with rules, adherence to which was almost as important as the racing they governed. Prizes were restricted to gold medals for the athletes and a plaque or silk banner for the winning club. Officially, the title was the Canadian Henley, to which the "Royal" prefix was added after 1908.[8]

In the early years each club had an opportunity to host this regatta, but in 1903 the association adopted the Martindale Pond in St. Catharines, Ontario, as a permanent site. Conveniently located near the entrance to the Welland Canal, access could be gained by water from Lake Ontario or by rail.

Over the years the site was developed, and in 1970 FISA accepted it for the hosting of the third World Championship. By 1992 the five-day event attracted over a hundred clubs and more than two thousand athletes from four continents. But in 1880 these developments still lay ahead.

The effects of the split from professionalism were predictable: the professionals continued rowing for the high financial rewards, and the amateurs rowed for glory and silver-plated trophies. For a while, the general public continued to follow the exploits of the professionals. By the turn of the century, however, their loyalties switched to the amateurs.

In Europe amateur associations were also formed. In 1892 five countries, Switzerland, Belgium, Italy, Holland and France, founded an international association: the Fédération International des Societés d'Aviron (FISA). For almost a century, however, the sport would remain the preserve of Europe, Australasia and North America. Not until almost one hundred years after its establishment would FISA actively promote the sport in Asia, Africa and South America.

However, in severing any connection with the professionals, rowing standards dropped and amateur rowing soon became identified with lower performances. Realizing that a vital element had been taken out of the sport, some clubs quickly hired professional oarsmen as coaches. This opened a new career for the professionals after their racing days were done. Even so, the rowing athletes of a century ago had much to learn before their performances would again be worthy of note. Interestingly, today's oarsmen and -women have adopted as part of their training programs the regimen that the professionals long followed. Simply put, training requires that athletes "put on the miles," and so they do. Most present-day world-class oarsmen and -women row 150 to 200 kilometres or more a week, a routine that the professionals of a hundred years ago would have taken as acceptable. But it was not always so.

One turn-of-the-century guide suggested as a daily training regimen a light breakfast (not more than two pork chops) followed by light exercise such a lying in a hammock and reading; a short half-hour walk before lunch with enough effort to generate a light sweat; not more than two pints of beer for lunch, followed again by more light exercise. According to the guide the main training of the day should take place in the afternoon. It should include an hour's rowing and a short run, after which the athlete should submit to a bath and rubdown, one glass of whisky, two glasses of wine and one of port for supper, and not more than two cigars before going to bed. Most athletes of today would gladly adopt such a training routine, if it only worked!

There were also some differences in race conduct from what is expected today. One boat club included in its rules the edict that, while anything could be thrown at the opponents, nothing was permitted that could damage a boat, although the opposing crews could (somehow) be forced out of their craft.

Compared to the attraction of regattas at which the professionals raced, few amateur races other than those between schools or universities attracted much public interest. There was no longer any real competition for World Championship titles; there would be occasional interest, but the races were shadows of ones held in the latter quarter of the nineteenth century. By the start of the Second World War, there was no official world champion, nor was there even interest in challenging for the title. The title remained dormant until 1962, when it reappeared in Lucerne, Switzerland. In Europe, FISA organized a European Championship, but Canada did not participate in this event until 1973. North American Championships did not reappear

until 1967, when the first was held at St. Catharines, Ontario. Thus, Canadian rowers, who had dominated world sculling for two decades, were left with only the Olympic games and an annual regatta held in England as regular opportunities for rowing on the world scene. Canadian oarsmen quickly took advantage of these two opportunities.

Rowing was to be included at the first Olympic games, held in 1896 at Athens and organized by Baron Pierre de Coubertin. However, poor weather cancelled the regatta, and the first Olympic rowing took place four years later at the second games, held in Paris. Canadian oarsmen did not participate in either of these games because they were held in Europe and not yet recognized as the pinnacle of success to which an amateur athlete can aspire. However, in 1904 the third Olympic games were held in St. Louis, a venue with which Canadian oarsmen had, by this time, become familiar. But the expense of travelling to the American location with boats was too much for the European and Australian rowing communities, so the only foreign crew to participate with the American hosts was a Canadian eight from the Argonaut Club in Toronto. They came second. In 1908, in London, Canada came third in the coxless fours and the coxless pairs, where rowing was held on a well-established course on the Thames at Henley.

## The Henley Royal Regatta

In 1839 the English village of Henley on Thames hosted a regatta for the first time as a tourist attraction. It received royal patronage and thereafter was known as the Henley Royal Regatta. By the turn of the century, it was established as pre-eminent among amateur rowing events. It annually attracted nearly all the best amateurs in the world. Three events in particular were held in the highest esteem: the Diamonds Challenge Cup for Singles, the Steward's Cup for Fours, and the Grand Challenge Cup for Eights.

Canada had entered for the Steward's and the Grand on a few previous occasions, but had never won anything. Thus, for Canadian oarsmen, entering a race at the Henley Royal was their version of going on a crusade: the effort represented the highest level of fulfilment of the ideals of amateurism, but the chances of success were slim. Indeed, the regatta rules were set in a determined effort to preclude any suggestion of professionalism. Entries were accepted only from bona fide amateur rowing clubs, who had to certify that their members were in the truest sense amateurs. At one time this definition meant that an oarsman had not in any way earned a living from manual labour. Such a squeaky-clean definition of amateurism meant that the top amateur American sculler in 1947, John Kelly, was refused entry reportedly because he had worked for a while as a labourer in his father's Philadelphia brick factory. Only later was this rule relaxed.

The Henley Royal became a natural focus in the class-conscious social circles of Victorian England. It helped, of course, that most oarsmen came from the rich upper classes who were accustomed to the comforts of home even at fashionable events held on river banks in small country towns.

The citizens of Henley on Thames were only too pleased to meet the demand, and the annual event grew in fame. With fame came increasing interest among the competitors, and the regatta provided a forum for world-class competition that would only be challenged by the Olympic games in the second half of the twentieth century.

The races at the Henley Royal are conducted today as they have been for over one hundred and fifty years. A rigid competitive ladder is established whereby crews and scullers race two at a time along a narrow stretch of the Thames, between two log booms. These booms define the course and protect the racers from unwanted swells of other water traffic. The winner proceeds to the next step. The process takes a full week, but foreign crews have always been granted an exemption from the preliminary rounds. Into this environment in 1904 came a young unknown Canadian sculler by the name of Lou Scholes from the Don Rowing Club near Toronto, accompanied by his professional coach, Patrick Mulqueen.

## Lou Scholes

Canada and the world were more interested in the events of the Russo-Japanese war than in amateur rowing. Scholes's entry in the Diamond Sculls was almost ignored, even though the Diamonds were, until the advent of official World Championships in the 1970s, considered the unofficial amateur World Championship. Perhaps this lack of interest, which was in sharp contrast to the interest that had greeted Hanlan's and Gaudaur's attempts at winning the World Professional Championships, signalled that people were tired of the sport. Perhaps Scholes was given little chance of winning.

In England, Scholes was greeted with amused tolerance; as the trainer of the previous year's winner of the coveted trophy loudly proclaimed: "He is no match for the favourite." The reigning champion, F.S. Kelly, agreed after following Scholes in the referee's launch during the first heats. The prevailing opinion was that the race would be a very dull affair, and the odds were four to one on Kelly.

At the start of the semifinal, Kelly led by two lengths at the halfway mark and several fans, expecting no change from what had been predicted, took an early train home. Scholes put on a burst at the three-quarter mark to pass Kelly, who, though he made a great effort, stopped, exhausted, at the Pavilion well short of the finish line. Grudgingly, the rowing pundits and the London press acknowledged that the race had been one of the greatest ever seen. They admitted that Scholes was a perfect wonder and consoled themselves that if England was to lose the Diamonds, they would, at least, remain in the Empire. Next day, Scholes easily beat J. Cloutte in the finals.

Canada, surprised, went wild with joy. On his return to Toronto, which then had a population of 310,000, a reported 70,000 people turned out to welcome Scholes home. Once again, the Dominion had beaten England. After the welcome, however, Scholes retired from rowing.

Scholes's brief appearance on the Canadian rowing scene failed to herald any continuation of the dominance in sculling that Canada had enjoyed for two decades. Indeed, by world standards, Canadian sculling, despite one or two notable attempts, would suffer a decline over almost thirty years. But the same was not true for Canadian rowing in general. Three clubs produced sweep crews who for the two decades before the First World War would be serious contenders on the North American and, to some extent, the world scene. They were the Argonaut Rowing Club of Toronto, and the Winnipeg and the Ottawa rowing clubs.

*In 1904 Lou Scholes became the first Canadian to win the coveted Diamond Sculls trophy at the Henley Royal Regatta, then unofficial symbol of the World Championship for amateur scullers.* —Hockey Hall of Fame Collection NAC PA50487

## Joe Wright Sr.

The Argonaut Rowing Club was established in 1873 and quickly built its reputation on the long tradition of rowing already found in the Toronto area. One of the earliest members of the club was a young Joseph Wright, who at the age of eighteen, began his rowing career that would see him forge an unbeaten record of over one hundred and thirty titles in singles, doubles and four-oared shells. In 1889 Wright turned to coaching, where he carried his personal success over to club crews, not only by coaching but also by rowing in many of the crews under his guidance for a further twenty years. This practice became his trademark: he would coach and simultaneously row—until World War I put a temporary stop to rowing on the world scene.

Wright's first success as a coach occurred in 1896 when he coached the senior and intermediate eights to win at a Baltimore regatta, all while stroking the senior eight. For a thirty-two-year-old athlete, the feat of winning was noteworthy in itself, but it was also remarkable that the two Argonaut crews were the only crews coached by an amateur coach at a time when the employment of professional coaches with worldwide reputations was common.

In the years before the war, the Argonauts, under Wright, went over to England five times to compete in the Henley Royal Regatta. In 1906, at the age of forty-three, he stroked the crew through two victories before being beaten by a distance of 6 feet in their third race, the semifinals of the Grand Challenge Cup. In 1913 the crew came the closest they ever would come to winning this prestigious trophy, but they were narrowly defeated in the final.

Even though the crew never managed to win at the Henley Royal Regatta, they had rather better success in the Olympic games. The Argonaut crews were selected for the 1904, 1908 and 1912 Olympics, again with Wright as both coach and stroke. In 1904 the crew went on to bring back a silver medal, even though the rowing part of the games was truncated by the fact that only two countries participated. In 1912, at Stockholm, the King of Sweden was so impressed with the crew and the coach that a special medal presentation was arranged. As one fan would later write: "The Argonauts in every way represented the best rowing traditions in the Dominion." But they were not alone.

## The Winnipeg Rowing Club and Con Riley

While the Argonauts reigned supreme in Eastern Canada, in Western Canada another club was emerging as a serious challenger to this domination. The Winnipeg Rowing Club was started in 1881 by a former Argonaut Rowing Club member, George Galt, and quickly established itself as one of the strongest clubs on the continent.

It was a time when rowing clubs were separated by considerable distances. The only reasonable means by which a club could compete against another was by travelling by train, taking their boats with them.[9] Special excursion trains were laid on so that fans could go to the regatta. But the east-west railway system in Canada was not fully developed: the Transcontinental had been completed only a scant decade before. On the other hand, railways to the United States, built to accommodate the north-south traffic, which had historically developed along the rivers in the regions, were well established. The result was that competition in North America developed along two axes: Toronto and the Eastern United States, and Winnipeg and the Midwest. The Pacific area would not become a serious contender until the new century.

As early as 1887 the Winnipeg Rowing Club started to win and by 1888 they were Canadian champions. In 1889 a young man, Conrad Riley, destined to become stroke of the club's most successful crew and later patron of the club, noted a red broom on the side of one of the Winnipeg buildings, with a banner proclaiming "a clean sweep." It marked the occasion of the club's victory in the United States Championship at Pullman, Illinois, by winning almost all events. It was a humbling experience for the Americans, but one that Canadians have continued to administer from time to time throughout the history of the sport.

In 1894 Winnipeg made its first attempt at winning at the Henley Royal and reached the finals of the Steward's Cup.

In 1904 the club again made plans to attend the Henley Royal. A boat was specially built for the crew and was loaded onto a railway flat car and sent via Liverpool to London. On the way, however, sparks from the engine dropped onto the canvas cover of the boat and set it alight. Enough of the boat was saved that it could be repaired and used in the race for the Steward's

Cup. But they were beaten by a length and a half by a crew from Trinity College, Cambridge, who equalled the course record set seven years earlier. Despite the disappointment of the race, the visit to England was memorable, since they were invited to visit Lord Strathcona in his English country home.

In 1909 the club again tried for the Steward's Cup, and this time Winnipeg won by several lengths and so became the first Canadian crew to succeed at this prestigious regatta. The win was celebrated in a typical Canadian style. At the inn where the Canadians were staying, a policeman was placed on special duty during the victory celebration; next morning his tunic and helmet were found hanging on a tree, while he had been safely put to bed. Civic receptions and dinners followed upon their return home.

In 1913 the club entered the Grand Challenge for eights, but were beaten by Harvard in the semifinal. Harvard went on to win. This Harvard crew met again in 1964 and rowed over the course in the exact same composition, even to the spare man still waiting to get into the boat. By then the boat reportedly had two bishops and a senator in its crew!

## The Ottawa Rowing Club

The one other club that challenged both the Argonaut and Winnipeg rowing clubs was the Ottawa club. The first of the three clubs to be established, it was founded in a local saloon on June 6, 1867, three weeks before the creation of Canada and some twelve years after rowing had started on the Ottawa River. The club claimed as its first honourary president the Prime Minister of Canada, Sir John A. Macdonald, and the mayor of Ottawa as its first honourary vice-president. The club continues to ask the prime minister and the mayor to fill those positions.[10]

The Ottawa club made its mark in the first year of its existence: the club four was the first crew on Canadian waters to row a four without a coxswain and retained the Canadian Championship by winning at Toronto. At the same regatta, the club's amateur sculler, Richard Haycock, beat professionals Berry and Tinning in the single sculls. Thereafter, for almost the next forty years of its existence, Ottawa was largely dormant, although it did host the Canadian Henley (the then unofficial national championships) in 1901.

The original clubhouse was built on pontoons and moored near the entrance to the Rideau Canal. Its location was poor, because every year, on the break-up of the ice on the river, the clubhouse would be ripped from its moorings and drift down river. In 1896 a permanent site for the club was established at the place where the drifting clubhouse usually came to rest, and a permanent clubhouse was built there that is still in use today. The club engaged professional coaches, many of whom had established world reputations. Hanlan, Wise, Stevenson of Australia, Ten Eyck and Rice all appeared at the Ottawa club, and its membership rose to one hundred and fifty six. In 1904, however, new crews appeared on the scene, and over the next five years they managed to win several Canadian and United States championships in eights and fours. In 1911, supported by the Ottawa community, the crew went to England and tried for the Grand Challenge Cup, but was unsuccessful. At the start of the First World War, Ottawa sank from the national scene and would not appear again as a major contender.

During the war, international rowing all but ceased, although the Canadian Henley was held every year but one.[11]

## Hilton Belyea

When the war was over, the focus of Canadian rowing shifted back to sculling in the Maritimes. There, Hilton Belyea, born in 1885 in Saint John, New Brunswick, began his rowing career at the age of thirty-five, an age at which most rowers would be finished with competition. He was reputedly unorthodox in many ways, and is said to have rowed with a bottle of rum hanging around his neck so as to replace fluids lost in sweating from exertion. His first win was at the Maritime Sculling Championship at Shediac, after which, in 1921, he broke into the international scene by winning the New England Championships on the Charles River in Boston. He then went to the Royal Canadian Henley, taking with him a homemade boat built by his brother Harry, a set of outrageous 17- inch sculls, and $1,600 in betting money. His arrival made quite a stir among the established rowing elite. To put it in a nutshell: he was too old, the boat was too heavy, his sculls were far too large, and he rowed a short sharp style some four strokes to the minute faster than anyone else.

Matched against Bob Dibble, the 1920 champion, Belyea sprang to the lead and won the title. In 1922 he repeated his win before going on to the United States Championships, where he narrowly lost to Paul Costello, the 1920 Olympic gold medallist. The next year he entered the Diamond Sculls but was defeated in the semifinals, after which he had to settle for second place at the Canadian Henley. It seemed that old age and heavy travelling were at last catching up with him. Nevertheless, he would not give up, and in 1924 he was selected to represent Canada at the Olympic games in Paris.

All went well until he suffered a sharp pain in his leg, diagnosed as a case of neuritis, despite which he rowed to the point where he had to be lifted in and out of the boat. Although he did not win a medal, the French officials were so impressed by his dogged determination that they awarded him a special bronze medal. It marked the end of his career and, in 1927, after a few more local wins, he hung up his sculls for good and made room for the arrival of two young scullers, Joe Wright Jr. (son of Joe Wright Sr.) and Jack Guest.

## Joe Wright Jr. and Jack Guest

During the war, Joe Wright Sr. moved to Philadelphia, where he coached successfully at the University of Pennsylvania. He remained there for the duration of the war and only returned in 1927, when his son Joe Jr. stated his intention to compete for the Diamonds, but rowing under Argonaut colours. On taking up his duties at the Argonauts, he also coached the senior eight and Jack Guest.

In 1939 Joe Wright's eight again came second in the Grand Challenge at the Henley Royal Regatta. The Second World War interrupted further international rowing, and Joe Wright Sr. gave up coaching at this level. In 1950, at the age of eighty-six, Joe Wright, a member of Canada's Sports Hall of Fame, passed away, leaving a legacy of excellence. He had started his athletic career at age thirteen by winning a sculling race, following which he expanded his interests to include boxing, football, baseball, track and field, wrestling and billiards.

As a boxer, Wright went on to win the Canadian Heavyweight Championship at the age of thirty-five. In senior football,

he played eighteen years for the Argonaut Football Club. While in baseball, he pitched the University of Toronto team to victories over Cornell and other U.S. College nines during a term in which Varsity never lost a game. Wright also excelled in track and field, achieving a record shot-put of 92 feet under the old rules of a stiff handle. He was the first Canadian to run 100 yards in ten seconds and the quarter mile in 53.5 seconds. He also won titles in amateur heavyweight wrestling and in billiards. It was a sporting career that earned him the title of Best Canadian Athlete of the First Half of the Twentieth Century.

Joe Wright Jr. was the youngest of "Mr. Joe's" five children and quickly followed in his father's footsteps by starting to row at the age of seventeen after wandering down to the Argonaut Rowing Club. He wasn't pushed into the sport, but assumed the "right of Wrights" as a natural undertaking and quickly established himself as a worthy oarsman. Standing 6 foot 4 inches and weighing between 190 and 210 pounds, for rowing and football respectively, he stroked the winning Argonaut eights in the Junior and Senior events at the 1923 Canadian Henley.

In 1927 young Joe departed with his father as coach for Henley on Thames, England, to challenge for the Diamonds.

In the finals, Joe was leading by about one length, when with only 10 yards to go, Joe's left scull became entangled in a rope dangling from one of the punts that formed the boom along the side of the course. His opponent forged ahead to win. So close to victory was he that the judges had already written "Wright wins" on their official course cards. His defeat, later described by Henley officials as "the most pathetic incident the Royal regatta has witnessed," was the greatest sensation of the 1927 Royal Henley Regatta, but he refused to regard it as anything more than a temporary setback. He returned to Canada and won both the Canadian and U.S. Senior Singles Championships. The Junior and Intermediate Championships were won by Jack Guest. It was inevitable that Joe and Jack's paths would soon cross, and in the spring of 1928 they started training alongside each other, with the Diamond Sculls and the Olympic games in mind.

Once in England, the two scullers followed a training schedule that was hard even by today's standards: under the watchful eye of Joe Sr. they would undertake two training sessions a day

*Jack Guest Sr., and Joe Wright Jr. From 1927 to 1930 these two Canadian scullers dominated the amateur rowing world by winning the Diamond Sculls, in 1930 and 1928 respectively. As a team they won the silver medal for double sculls in the 1928 Olympic games.* —NAC PA151013

for a total of 8 to 9 miles. Young Joe, with his towering physique, was considered the most powerful sculler witnessed at the Henley Royal in many years, but was less proficient technically than Guest. Still, even though Guest's technique was much better, more smooth and efficient, Joe was the favoured one.

The luck of the draw and the results of the preliminary heats prevented a meeting between the two Canadians until the semifinals. Just after the start of the race between them, Jack hit the outside boom, and Joe, seeing his predicament, stopped rowing until Jack was clear again. Before a crowd of eighty thousand enthusiasts, Joe defeated Jack by half a length in a race considered to be "a classic example of true sportsmanship." In the final, Joe edged Robert Lee of Oxford to become the second Canadian to win the elusive Diamonds. After that, together with Jack, he won a silver medal at the 1928 Amsterdam Olympic games. The other Canadian crew trained by Joe Wright Sr., the eight, also won a silver medal.

In 1929 Jack Guest left to train in England in preparation for the Henley Royal, and Joe soon followed, in an attempt to become the first Canadian to win the Diamonds twice in succession. Again, the two would meet before the finals, and again Joe, with 50 yards to go, and Jack having held the lead for most of the $1\frac{1}{2}$-mile race, put on a frantic burst of speed to win by one quarter of a length. Most observers felt that the outcome of the race between Jack and Joe would be the factor in deciding the winner of the Diamonds, but a diminutive Dutch ironworker by the name of Berthen Gunther, who had advanced quite readily through the preliminary races, managed to win by a scant 3 feet in a crowd-pleasing final.

From 1930 on, Joe's rowing career became what might be described as inconsistent. At the 1930 English Henley, he was beaten in the semifinals by the German sculler, Boetzelen, who in the finals lost to Jack Guest by thirty lengths in one of the most lopsided victories in the history of the Henley. The win was Jack's last race because, as he said, "Once you get the Diamonds, you should be satisfied." For some, his brief but spectacular career in rowing would be regarded as a flash in the pan, but to most oarsmen, Jack epitomized the image of the amateur sculler for whom technical excellence and glorious success is what the sport is all about.

Joe quickly returned home from the 1930 Henley to represent Canada at the British Empire Games held the following weekend at Hamilton and was beaten by the indomitable Australian, Bobby Pearce.

## Robert Pearce

For many sports historians, Bobby Pearce is considered the greatest sculler of the period. He won three national championships and two Olympic gold medals (Amsterdam in 1928 and Los Angeles in 1932) for his native land. He was considered unbeatable, and his strength and low stroke rates were legendary.

Pearce, rowing for his Canadian club, Leander, won the Diamond Sculls in 1931, and after his win at the 1932 Los Angeles Games turned professional. In 1933 he beat the reigning British and world champion Phelps for the world title.

Pearce was reputedly a colourful man who loved, among other things, to gamble. On one visit to Vancouver, to cover his losses, he sold to a member of the Vancouver Rowing Club a diamond-studded cane that Ned Hanlan had given him.

The outbreak of World War II put an end to his career, and Pearce retired as the only sculler never defeated as both amateur and professional world champion.

With the retirements of Joe Wright Jr., Jack Guest and Bobby Pearce, an important era in Canadian sculling came to an end. Not for fifty years would Canada again produce scullers who could seriously challenge on the world scene.

In the meantime, international rowing stopped to accommodate the Second World War.

# AFTER THE SECOND WORLD WAR

After the second World War was over, rowing, like so many sports, started to rebuild. In Europe, FISA reestablished its European championships for men and, pressed by the French and Dutch federations, considered the introduction of championships for women. The debate over women lasted for seven years, until 1953, when FISA finally agreed to hold the first women's championships in 1954. One condition, however, was that the championships could be held before or after, but not together with the men's event. In Canada there was no response to the European initiative, although women had rowed at St. Catharines as early as 1947.

Canada, too, rebuilt rowing after the war, but conditions had changed, and so the effort was split along geographic lines into two very different streams.

Too many young men of rowing age had served in the war and, on returning to Canada, wanted to catch up on the years they had missed. They competed for scarce shells and even scarcer coaching. It was not a happy mix, because not only was there a difference in ages, there was also a difference in the attitudes of the athletes; the result was to generate an almost clean break between the prewar and the postwar traditions and the continuity between generations that had always characterized the sport. However, the rupture could be healed, and healed it was in two main locations: St. Catharines in the East and Vancouver in the West.

## The St. Catharines Rowing Club

At St. Catharines, rowing focussed on high-school students and was supported by the business community in a manner unequalled elsewhere in the country. Steps were taken to acquire land on which to build boathouses and docks. With community support, funds were found to acquire boats, and coaches were found to train the young athletes. Competition between the local schools was fostered and became very keen. Soon, the venerable

Martindale Pond was covered with eights as over seven hundred students participated in what became an annual spring rite, the Canadian Secondary Schools Rowing Association Championships. Thus began a tradition which has continued to this day and still occupies many of the athletes who started rowing in those days. It was a tradition on which rowing in Ontario was able to reestablish itself after the war.

## The Vancouver Rowing Club and Frank Read

In the West, the approach was somewhat different. The long-established Vancouver Rowing Club found itself with the expertise and the facilities but without athletes, while the University of British Columbia was full of prime athletes but had no rowing traditions. When Vancouver was chosen for the 1954 Commonwealth Games, conditions seemed right for the two to join forces. From this joint venture came the UBC/VRC crews and a new and unexpected force in rowing.

Local rowing supporters persuaded a hotel owner, Frank Read, to coach the new joint-venture crews. He was a gruff individual, known for refusing to mince his words or guard his comments. But he could coach and he could bring out the best in his athletes. While some people cringed at his public expressions, his athletes and the rowing community revered him.

Read started on an arduous training program that covered hundreds of miles over the choppy driftwood-strewn waters of Coal Harbour. His intensive program, often leading as far as the Second Narrows Bridge in all kinds of weather, morning and evening, soon began to produce results.

The first to suffer the consequences of Read's training programs were the crews from the universities of Oregon and Washington. To their horror and surprise an unknown force had appeared on the West Coast and soon began to threaten and then demolish what hitherto had been an American preserve. When the crews met, if the UBC/VRC eight did not win, they still managed to give their rivals a painful and exhausting challenge to remember. By the opening of the Commonwealth Games, Vancouver's rowing community was quietly confident that the Canadian eight would surprise the world.

The 1954 Commonwealth Games teams arrived in mid-July, but attention was focussed on track and field, where, it was rumoured, an Englishman named Roger Bannister was going to try to run the mile in four minutes or less. As far as the Canadian public knew, rowing would not be one of the exciting events for Canada. Bannister did break the 4-minute mile, but the biggest upset of the games occurred when the Canadian eight, generally considered a crew of green kids, finished the 2000-metre course two and a half lengths ahead of Thames Rowing Club, the English crew. As the official history of the Games told it: "The crowd was literally stunned by the fantastic victory and limp from excitement."

For the first time ever, Canada had won a gold medal for eights in international competition beyond competition, with the Americans.

After the final race, the Duke of Edinburgh met with the chairman of the VRC rowing committee, Nelles Stacey, and asked what the club owed its victory to. The answer came back: "Frank Read, Frank Read, Frank Read." Intrigued, the Duke asked to meet Read and said, "You must come to Henley." Read was not impressed, but the rest of the VRC committee took it as a royal command, and training and preparation followed until the crew left for England and the Grand Challenge Cup.

The 1950s had seen the resurgence of rowing in all countries, not the least of which was the then Soviet Union. There, sport had become a political tool in the Cold War, designed to show, through the excellence of its athletes, that the Communist way was superior to the way of the West. Their efforts had included rowing, and in 1954 they had appeared at the Henley Royal and gone home with all the titles. It was, to say the least, embarrassing, and no one seemed able to do anything about it. In 1955 the invasion by these seemingly "professional" state-subsidized oarsmen happened again and left the guardians of amateur sport, the Henley stewards, shaking their heads in dismay. Still, some hope existed; after all, this unknown crew, which had just won the gold medal at the Commonwealth Games, was entered

and, though the Soviets were heavily favoured, miracles did occasionally happen.

For the Canadian rowing club, the experience was not without hazards; their shell was caught in the middle of a British dock strike. Canadian and British officials tried their best, but the unions were unyielding and the boat was not released until the dispute had been settled. Meanwhile, the shell suffered the ravages of weeks of weathering and was no longer rowable. UBC/VRC used a borrowed boat.

UBC/VRC met Krasnoe Znamia, the Russian club, in the semifinals, where the Soviets quickly jumped into a three-quarter-length lead. At the quarter mile, the Russians dropped their rate to thirty-six, Vancouver to thirty-three. At the half-mile post the Russian lead was cut to 6 feet, and by the three-quarters mark, the Canadians were leading by 6 feet. When that position was announced, the vast crowd, expecting an easy Russian win, rose to its feet with a roar. To an ever-increasing din, the Vancouver crew rowed on to win by one and a half lengths. The Russians surrounded the victorious crew and marvelled at the style of "coming off the feather at the last moment." They called it the Read stroke and wondered, as do all losing crews, whether this was the secret of the Canadians' success. The real secret, of course, was dedication, discipline and physical conditioning.

Nelles Stacey later stated that there were three records set that day at Henley: "Never had there been such wild cheering by a Henley crowd; never had the staid Henley stewards been seen to throw their caps in the air; and never before, during a race, had all the bars been empty."

In the final the next day against the University of Pennsylvania, the crew lost by a third of a length in what was described as one of the finest races of the day. The loss was greeted as a victory: The House of Commons sent their congratulations, the mayor of Vancouver greeted them on arrival and gave them a motor parade through the city, followed by a formal address on the courthouse steps. Each member of the crew received a gold medal in recognition of their fine showing.

After this, the next challenge was the 1956 Olympic games in Melbourne, Australia. As a result of the strenuous training program, the crew rowed over 1,250 miles in three months. But this gave no hint of what was to come. Virtually unnoticed training

*Canada's Olympic gold-medal-winning four-oared crew, 1956. From the Vancouver Rowing Club, left to right: Archie McKinnon, Lorne Loomer, Walter d'Hondt, Don Arnold.*
—Hockey Hall of Fame Collection NAC PA50476

alongside the eight, and given little chance for success, was a coxless four stroked by Don Arnold, with Walter d'Hondt, Lorne Loomer and Archie MacKinnon, coached by assistant coach John Warren. Frank Read remarked: "They don't look like much, but they sure move the boat." Still, they were not remarkable enough to be included in the Canadian Olympic Association's plans for an eleven-man team. Only by promising to underwrite the costs of the trip was the Vancouver Rowing Committee able to finally persuade the COA to let the four go.

In the first heat on Lake Ballarat, 50 miles north of Melbourne, the four beat Germany by six lengths, with Australia and Denmark behind. In the semifinals, the winning margin was an astounding ten lengths over France, Russia and Poland. The eight, meanwhile, finished second to Australia in the first heat and sent the Americans to the repechage (a second chance to qualify) in a stunning upset.

In the finals, the four went out and beat the United States by five lengths, with Italy and France following. It was Canada's first ever Olympic gold medal in rowing.

How close the eight came to winning another gold medal will always be a matter of speculation. The Americans won by half a length, but three of their oarsmen collapsed and two required medical attention. Truly, it was a performance in the highest traditions of the Olympic spirit. It was also a sweet vindication for the efforts to convince the COA.

On their return to a justifiably proud Vancouver, someone in the crowd asked Read, "When did you think they were going to win?" Read's reply, "When they left the boathouse."

Read coached again for the 1960 Olympic games, held in Rome. There, the race in the final for the eights became a battle between Canada and (at that time) West Germany, with a crew from the German rowing academy at Ratzeburg. With 200 metres to go, the Ratzeburg crew put on a magnificent spurt to win by four seconds. Canada's silver medal was the only medal

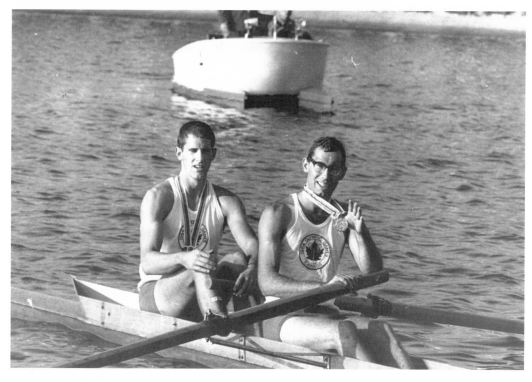

*George Hungerford and Roger Jackson display their gold medals after winning the Coxless Rowing Pairs at the 1964 Olympics in Tokyo.*

—Hockey Hall of Fame Collection NAC PA50390

Canada won at the Rome Olympics. It also marked the end of the Frank Read era.

The 1964 Olympic games were held in Tokyo, and again VRC/UBC formed the major part of the Canadian rowing team. Glen Mervyn had taken over from Frank Read as head coach. All was going according to plan when George Hungerford, in the number-three seat of the eight, fell victim to mononucleosis.

After three weeks in bed, Hungerford returned and, having lost his place in the eight, trained for the remaining two weeks in the pair with a relative novice, Roger Jackson. This would prove to be a tale that no rowing man would believe.

Two men, one of whom was only recently recovering from mononucleosis, rowing together for just two weeks, entered their first official race, which happened to be an Olympic heat, and won. They went straight to the final to win a gold medal.

The eight, looking for a medal, finished ninth.

The gold medal in Tokyo was, for the next fifteen years, the only success of Canadian rowing on the world stage. At Mexico in 1968, Munich in 1972, and Montreal in 1976, Canadian national rowing teams fared poorly. A change was necessary. That change came in the way Canadian rowing prepared itself for international competition.

For over a century, oarsmen had been encouraged or enticed to join a specific club, where they trained to represent Canada. The club would undertake all the preparation considered necessary for the athletes to compete in selection regattas or trials. The winners of these trials would then represent Canada in their events at the next world competition. In 1968 the last of these trials took place and a small team went to Mexico for the Olympics.

# THE CHANGE

After 1968, influenced by several coaches, such as Martin Bielz and Tudor Bompa, both from Rumania, Chris Korzienowski from Poland and Peter Klavora from Yugoslavia, Canada followed the European example of selecting the best athletes and boating them into composite crews. A composite crew is made up of members who may have trained at different clubs or locations and who have come together shortly before an event to train as a crew.

An additional change took place when women finally joined the Canadian rowing fraternity. Women were welcomed into the Canadian rowing fraternity in 1971 as equal members. In 1973 Canada sent its first ever women's contingent to an international championship when a coxed four from Victoria, coached by Wayne van Osterhout, and a double from Montreal, coached by Harry Goetschi, entered in the European championships in Moscow. They did not do very well, but it was important that they were there.

The following year the Canadian Association of Amateur Oarsmen changed its name to the Canadian Amateur Rowing Association to recognize that women were equal members.

The change in Canada was not welcomed by all. One long-standing member of one of the oldest clubs was heard to loudly proclaim that women would enter his club "only over my dead body." Ironically, the women's crew of his club are, at the time of writing, leaders on the domestic rowing scene in Canada, just as the men were when he himself rowed.

In 1976 women's rowing was included at the Montreal Olympics and the separation of the sexes was closed. The games were a disappointment for Canadian rowing, where the best result was a fifth-place finish in the men's four without coxswain. At the World Lightweight Championships held in Montreal in 1984, women, who had hitherto rowed only 1,000 metres, for the first time rowed the same 2,000-metre course as the men, and the battle of the sexes was largely over.

The introduction of women into the sport, and the appearance in Canada of coaches from the Communist countries, changed more than just the composition of crews and who could row. Techniques of rowing and the preparation of athletes were also affected. But here, Canada did have experience and a tradition of success. Not only had Canadians done well internationally, but there was also a good club system in place producing talented athletes from whom crews could be selected. A debate began on how far the ideas imported with the new coaches should be allowed to intrude into the existing rowing scene. Canadian experience and imported expertise had to mix and lessons had to be learned.

## Neil Campbell

Into this process, success suddenly came from an entirely new area. At St. Catharines, where schoolboy rowing had taken a firm hold, there appeared a new force to be reckoned with.

Ridley College, one of Canada's prestigious private schools, asked Neil Campbell, who at thirty-nine had stroked the 1968 Olympic eight, to coach. His crew won the championship eights at the Canadian and the United States high-school championships and then went to the Henley Royal Regatta to win the Princess Elizabeth Challenge Cup, symbol of preeminence in British high-school rowing. It was the first cup for eights Canada brought home from this regatta. Over the rest of the decade, Campbell's crews would bring home the Henley Royal trophy no less than five times. Canada had found a new source of pride.

Campbell started rowing at the St. Catharines Rowing Club at age twenty-two. Having rowed for his father's boat livery, he was accustomed to rowing groups of fishermen out onto Lake Ontario; that and his 240-pound frame made him a natural oarsman. He made the Olympic teams of 1964 and 1968, after which he retired from active competition to coach. Years later, he was recognized as having a unique ability that could turn almost any group of oarsmen into a championship crew. One of his former oarsmen said of him: "He knows what it takes to make a national champion, and he won't accept less." Beneath his somewhat gruff exterior was a competitor who could assess what it took to win, and an emotional spark plug who could motivate a crew to work like a well-tuned engine. It was not so much that he wanted to win, he just hated to lose. Another coach was ready to stand next to the by-now legendary Frank Read.

As Campbell's crews were winning at the schoolboy level, the changes on the national scene that had been introduced over the past eight years bore fruit. In 1977 the first truly composite crew, a women's eight, entered the World Championships. Comprised of athletes from clubs in Ontario and British Columbia, they went on to win Canada's first medal for women, a bronze. It was the start of almost two decades of unbroken medal-winning performances during which women were to bring back gold, silver or bronze medals from almost every international championships. They established a record the men have not yet been able to equal.

## Rudi Wieler

After the 1977 bronze medal, a women's eight won another bronze at the 1978 World Championships. Next, a St. Catharines high-school teacher, Rudi Wieler, who himself had never rowed, undertook to coach junior women's crews for the Junior World Championships to be held in 1979 in Moscow.

In the finals, the Canadian eight was in the lead, but only by a second at the point where, traditionally, the Eastern bloc countries would make their move and snatch victory from defeat. Indeed, the Soviets started to make their move and tried to overtake Canada, but failed. The decade during which the Eastern countries had dominated junior rowing ended on the Soviet home course. Canada won by half a second over the Soviet Union and a second and a half over the East German crews. It was Canada's first ever gold medal in eights in world competition.

## The 1980 and 1984 Olympics

The Canadians saw the 1980 Olympic games as a chance to display the success of the composite approach to boating crews, and there was great anticipation of results. The training plan was considered excellent and crews eagerly prepared for the trip to Moscow. In the end it was not to be, as world politics prompted a boycott by the Western nations. The Canadian crews were bitterly disappointed. Eight years later, one athlete was to say, "Those of us who retired will never know how we would have done against the rest of the world in our last major competition. We trained, we had to qualify in trials to go to Europe and to qualify for the Olympic team in competitions in Lucerne and Amsterdam. But that's all it was, training and qualification. On paper, we made the team, and that to me, at least, means that we were good enough." Another asked, "How were we to be judged and compensated for our investment in the Olympic program?"

As 1984 started, politics again interfered as the Eastern European countries boycotted the Los Angeles Olympic games. But in June prior to the games, at the Rotsee Regatta in Lucerne, Switzerland, all countries except the Soviet Union appeared at what has traditionally been regarded as the pre-Olympic testing regatta. Canada's entry in the eight was coached by Neil Campbell.

In its first race, the Canadians felt a quiet determination and conviction that "this would be it." When the Canadians and the Americans each won one race, it became quite clear that the race for the gold at Los Angeles would be between these two crews.

Lake Casitas is a picturesque lake on the outskirts of Los Angeles, where no motorboats are allowed because it is a protected natural habitat. Placid in the morning, the prevailing winds gather force as the day draws on, so that by noon there is an unhealthy chop that makes racing difficult. Racing thus took place in the morning.

As expected, Canada and the United States were close to each other under starter's order for the grand final of the men's eights. Immediately the flag moved to signify the start. Canada surged ahead and had established a three-quarters-of-a-boat's-length lead by the halfway mark. Excitement mounted in the grandstand as it dawned on the Canadian contingent that a

*Men's eight crew celebrating their gold medal in the 1984 Olympics at Los Angeles.* —Ted Grant, Canadian Sports Images

dream was about to come true. The American crowd, seeing that the home team was lying second but within striking distance of winning, began to roar encouragement. As the noise increased it was clear that the Americans must make their move soon. With about 200 metres to go, the Americans took up the power and the rate. Initially, there seemed to be no effect, but then the American bow started to appreciably catch up to the Canadians. Noting that the Americans were beginning to sprint, the Canadians put in their own effort and, to the frenzied roar of the crowd, the Canadian eight strained to hold off the challenge. At first, it looked as if it would work, but then, inexorably, the Americans moved up, gaining a seat (about 2 feet) every two strokes. As the American bow crept up from four seat, to three, to two, to bow, no one noticed in the excitement that the Canadian bow had crossed the finish line, a good 6 feet ahead of the American boat. Canada had its first gold medal in the eights at the Olympic games.

In the end, Canada came home with six medals, its best-ever performance. In addition to the gold, the men's crews brought home a bronze in the quad and in the singles (Bob Mills of North Star). In the women's events, crews brought home three silver medals: the women's four with cox, the women's double (Danielle and Silken Laumann) and the women's pair (Betty Craig and Tricia Smith). For Betty Craig, the results were not what she had hoped for. After winning five silver and bronze medals in world competition, the gold would still elude her.

## Jack Nicholson

No one really expected that the euphoria of the Olympic gold medal could be sustained. However, under the coaching of Jack Nicholson, the quadruple sculls crew of Paul Douma, Doug Hamilton, Mel Laforme and Bob Mills brought back the gold from the 1985 World Championships. Defying a tricky tailwind on the Hazewinkel, Belgium, course the Canadian quad jumped to an early lead and were able to win over East Germany by a 2-foot length.

Jack Nicholson was a seven-year veteran of national team coaching who had spent over thirty-five years on the rowing course at St. Catharines. He started rowing as a teenager and within two years had won his first Henley gold medal. Starting

in the early 1960s, and for the next seventeen years, he coached a variety of crews before moving to the Ridley Graduates Boat Club in 1971. Ten years later he became one of Canada's national team coaches, concentrating on sculling.

A reticent person, Nicholson could usually be seen in the boathouse, wearing a white floppy hat, rigging shells. Perhaps his philosophy could be summed up in his answer to one questioner about his chances at an upcoming event: "Well," he said with a grin," I'm not here to lose."

At the 1987 World Championships, the lightweight scullers carried on the winning traditions. Heather Hattin and Janice Mason won the gold in the lightweight women's sculls, while Dave Wright of St. Catharines brought back a silver.

The men's quad finished third, for the second straight year. For three consecutive years, the four oarsmen, coached by Jack Nicholson, had finished in the medals. It was a remarkable feat, but it was also the beginning of the end.

## The 1988 Olympics

The 1988 Olympic games in Seoul will be, for Canada, a poignant memory for years to come. Sprinter Ben Johnson, winner of the gold medal and holder of the world title in the 100 metres, was found to have used banned drugs and was stripped of his honours. The effect was traumatic for every Canadian, whether competing, present at the games, or watching at home on television. Mercifully lost in the media was the worst performance by Canadian crews in almost fifteen years. For the first time since 1974, Canadian crews not only failed to bring home a medal from international competition, but not one crew ended in the top six or top half of the entries. The future looked bleak.

## Al Morrow and Mike Spracklen

In 1989 two new coaches took up their positions: Mike Spracklen, who had completed a very successful career as a British national coach, trained the men and joined Al Morrow, a Canadian veteran oarsman, who trained the women. The first year in the new configuration proved a resounding success.

*Silken Laumann, undisputed women's world champion in sculling by winning in 1991 both the World Championship and the World Cup. In 1992, though hampered by a severe injury sustained ten weeks earlier, Silken won a bronze medal at the Olympic games.* —Dominik Keller

## Silken Laumann

At the 1990 World Championships, held in Tasmania, Canadian crews won gold in the lightweight women's four (Rachel Starr, Jill Blois, Diane Sinnege and Colleen Milles) and silver in the men's eight and the women's single sculls. In 1991, at the World Championships, the men's eight won the silver medal, while Canada was catapulted into first-ranked place in women's rowing in the world when all four entries returned with gold. Marnie McBean and Kathleen Heddle won the pair; Jessica Monroe, Brenda Taylor, Kirsten Baines and Jenny Doey the four; all six joined Megan Delehanty, Kelly Mahon and Lesley Thompson to win the eight. Easily identifiable among the cham-

pions was Silken Laumann, who not only won the World Championship but also the World Cup. (The World Cup is awarded on the basis of aggregating results of a series of specified competitions.) She became Canada's first world champion in singles sculling since Jack Guest had won the Diamond Sculls some sixty years earlier.

Silken first joined the national team in 1983 after rowing as a high-school novice that spring. From the start she was fast, although, as one report had it, she barely knew how to hold her sculls. A year later she teamed with her sister, Danielle, to win a bronze medal at the Olympics.

As one teammate was to write: "Silken's body is a glorious athletic instrument. She trains passionately, but not always within the bounds of good sense." She was described as a youthful Valkyrie, a Nordic warrior goddess with white hair and a smile that lit up her face like a 150-watt bulb. In this fine athlete Canada discovered its first rowing heroine ever.

Her successes at the 1990 and 1991 World Championships were warmly welcomed in a country still smarting from the disgrace of the steroid scandals of the 1988 Olympic games. In Silken, Canada found a wholesome athlete with whom the nation could identify and whose successes could not be measured in millions of dollars. As Silken increasingly became the focus of media attention, an unfamiliar warm feeling of pride developed in Canada. It was confidently expected that Silken and other athletes, such as decathlete Mike Smith, would redeem Canada's tarnished amateur sports image at the Barcelona Olympic games. International expectations were also high: Silken was expected to win the Olympic gold medal quite handily.

## The 1992 Olympics

As the countdown towards the Olympic games started, the spotlight on Silken increased in intensity. In their glare, the women's sweep crews and the men's eight were all but forgotten. Then, in March, at a regatta at Essen, Silken collided with a German pair and suffered severe injuries to her leg. Five operations were required in ten days to repair the damage, and it was considered likely she would not be going to the games.

The prophets of doom did not take Silken's determination into account. As the nation watched and waited, Silken retired to Victoria with her coach. There, with great determination, she decided to try to overcome her severe disadvantage. As she recuperated and recovered, there were weekly accounts of her progress. Not even royalty has had as much public attention given to an injury. She was first pronounced able to row, and then fit to go to Barcelona. Still, while going to the games was a tremendous achievement in itself, it fell far short of the medal everyone had hoped for.

At the opening of the games, Silken did not attend the ceremonies, preferring instead to rest her leg. Mike Smith carried the flag for Canada in the opening parade, and the Olympic games began. There was a current of excitement among Canadians, which burst forth when Mark Tewkesbury won a gold medal in swimming. He cited Silken's efforts as one of the inspirational factors. But the thrill was quickly subdued when Jennifer Doey, stroke of the women's four, suffered a back injury and was replaced by Kay Worthington, a spare, at the very last moment. Excitement mounted again when Marnie McBean and Kathleen Heddle won the pairs handily. It rose higher when Kay, Jessica Monroe, Brenda Taylor and Kirsten Barnes won the four to bring home Canada's third gold medal. It reached fever pitch when at 3 A.M. Eastern time Canadians got out of bed to watch the television coverage of Silken rowing in the finals. As expected, Silken did not lead at the start, but by the middle of the race, she had moved towards the lead and it became clear that she was in contention for a medal. She was rowing strongly, pushing Elizabeth Lipa of Rumania and holding off a challenging Annelies Braedel of Belgium. In the end, the effects of her injury began to tell and she could not catch up with the winner nor hold off a last-minute spurt from behind—but she won a bronze medal. For everyone, whether present at the course or watching at home, the sight of a superb athlete overcoming daunting odds was an emotional experience. Silken Laumann epitomized what an Olympic athlete should be.

Silken's race was a poignant moment that will not be forgotten, and the delirium of the event was quickly increased when the women's eight crewed by the same crew, except for Kay Worthington (in the place of the injured Jenny Doey) and Shannon Crawford (to replace Kelly Mahon), as had won the World Championship won their event by almost a length. Still, that was not all. Next day, the men's eight (Mike Forgeron, Robert Marland, Bruce Robertson, Derek Porter, Mike Rascher, John Wallace, Andy Crosby, Darren Barber and Terry Paul) jumped out to take the lead and, although Rumania made a worthy effort, Canada won the gold medal. It was, to say the least, a clean sweep. Canada had won four gold and one bronze medal at the same Olympic games.

There were several firsts: for the first time, Canadian women had won two gold medals at the same Olympic games; for the first time, Canadian women had won gold at the World Championships and the Olympic games consecutively; Al Morrow, coach of the women's crews, had coached six crews and won six gold medals over two years, a feat never before performed in rowing, by any coach anywhere. For Mike Spracklen, who despite his impressive coaching of British oarsmen had been denied the opportunity of coaching the British eight, the Olympic gold following on two consecutive World Championship silver medals was a sweet vindication of his ideas. Canada was undisputed leader in world rowing. Three medals at the World Lightweight and Junior Championships in Montreal added even more to the lustre of the Olympic successes.

## Three World-Champion Scullers

In 1992 world rowing again gathered for its annual championships, this time at Racice, in the newly established Czech Republic. Set in the Bohemian countryside, Racice's racecourse has been gouged out of the lush farmland, sadly neglected under years of centralized economic planning. In the distance, picturesque baroque villages could be seen beside monuments of Communist industrial mismanagement. Here, Canada's entries were largely untested. Only the straight fours included experienced members of the 1992 crews. The other sweep crews were rowing together for the first time and were not given much chance of winning a medal.

In sculling, Colleen Miller, Marnie McBean and Derek Porter, medallists in 1992, left the comfort of their sweep-crew boats and ventured into world-class sculling for the first time. Wendy Wiebe, Michelle Darville and Timothy Prince, though seasoned scullers, were on the world scene for the first time in their lightweight events. In the sweep events, there was hope that the women's four without cox would do well in both the lightweight and heavyweight events. There was some hope that the men's four without cox might do well, but other than that, expectations outside the Canadian camp were low.

In their heats, Marnie, Michelle and Derek all advanced to the next stage, as did Colleen Miller and Wendy Wiebe in the lightweight women's double. The three fours and the men's lightweight eight also advanced to the finals. Marnie McBean's chances improved when Elizabeth Lipa suffered a nosebleed during her race and failed to win. Derek Porter achieved the fastest time in his semifinal, but as rivals noted, times and competition can be deceptive, because athletes may relax once it is clear they have qualified for the finals.

By the day of the finals, the nervousness of some national teams became apparent. In the German camp, Thomas Lange, Olympic and five times World singles champion was concerned about this upstart Porter from Canada. In the Czech camp, there was confidence that the twice silver-medallist Vaclav Chalupa would win this time.

The day of the finals produced surprises. The Canadian lightweight women's single and double all rowed strongly to come in first, while the four came second to China. In the women's heavy four a last-minute sprint from the United States placed Canada third to China's win. Marnie McBean was unable to catch the German, but nevertheless brought home silver. In the lightweight men's eight (Chris Cookson, Robert Fontaine, Peter Somerwil, Jay Lay, David Boyes, Bryn Thompson, Greg Hasset, Brian Peaker and Pat Newman), Canada stayed with the favourite, the Italian eight, trailing by less than half a second for the first half of the race. Taking the lead at the 1,500-metre mark, Canada went on to win by almost a full boat length. It was Canada's first-ever gold medal men's lightweight sweep, a great feat achieved against all expectation.

In the men's single, Porter, Lange and Chalupa challenged each other for the first 1,800 metres, but then Lange began to fade. With Porter in the lead, Chalupa increased his pace and began overtake Porter. Through the sound of almost three thousand screaming supporters and the driving rain, it appeared that Chalupa had achieved his purpose. However, Porter was able to make the effort and hold off the challenge: Canada had its first official men's world champion since Jake Gaudaur, almost a century earlier.

When the regatta finished, Canada went home clearly the most successful nation, with four gold, two silver and one bronze; three more medals than the next nation, Great Britain, which had claimed four gold medals.

Canada had maintained its pre-eminence in that most beautiful of sports, the sport of rowing.

# WORLD MEDALS
## WON BY CANADIANS

| YEAR | EVENT | RESULT | RACE | CREW | CLUB |
|---|---|---|---|---|---|
| 1880 | WORLD CHAMPIONSHIP | GOLD | SINGLES | HANLAN, NED | TORONTO |
| 1881 | WORLD CHAMPIONSHIP | GOLD | SINGLES | HANLAN, NED | TORONTO |
| 1882 | WORLD CHAMPIONSHIP | GOLD | SINGLES | HANLAN, NED | TORONTO |
| 1884 | WORLD CHAMPIONSHIP | GOLD | SINGLES | HANLAN, NED | TORONTO |
| 1885 | HENLEY ROYAL | FINALIST | FOURS | HOGG, J. | ARGONAUT R.C. |
| | | | | THOMPSON, G. | |
| | | | | MORPHY, C. | |
| | | | | MCKAY, R. | |
| 1894 | HENLEY ROYAL | FINALIST | FOURS | MARKS, C. | WINNIPEG |
| | | | | OSBORNE, J. | |
| | | | | LLOYD, E. | |
| | | | | ARMITAGE, J.C.G. | |
| 1896 | WORLD CHAMPIONSHIP | GOLD | SINGLES | GAUDAUR, JAKE | ORILLIA |
| 1898 | WORLD CHAMPIONSHIP | GOLD | SINGLES | GAUDAUR, JAKE | ORILLIA |
| 1904 | HENLEY ROYAL | WIN | SINGLES | SCHOLES, LOU | DON |
| 1904 | HENLEY ROYAL | FINALIST | FOURS W/O COX | RILEY, C.S. | WINNIPEG |
| | | | | HENDERSON, J.S. | |
| | | | | KENT, A.H.E. | |
| | | | | HAMBERG, E.W. | |
| 1904 | OLYMPICS | SILVER | EIGHTS | BAILEY, J. | ARGONAUT |
| | | | | ALLEN, A. | |
| | | | | REIFENSTEIN, G. | |
| | | | | RICE, C. | |
| | | | | BURCHILL | |
| | | | | WADSWORTH | |
| | | | | MACKENZIE, D. | |
| | | | | WRIGHT SR., J. | |
| | | | | BESTEDO, N. (COX) | |
| 1908 | OLYMPICS | BRONZE | PAIRS W/O COX | TOMS, F. | ARGONAUT |
| | | | | JACKES, N. | |
| 1910 | HENLEY ROYAL | WIN | FOURS W/O COX | CARRUTHERS, F.F. | WINNIPEG |
| | | | | ALLEN, C.E. | |
| | | | | ALDOUS, G.B. | |
| | | | | RILEY, C.S. | |
| 1912 | OLYMPICS | SILVER | SINGLES | BUTLER, E. | ARGONAUT R.C. |
| 1913 | HENLEY ROYAL | FINALIST | EIGHTS | RIDDY, C. | ARGONAUT R.C. |
| | | | | WICKSON, G. | |
| | | | | KENT, P. | |
| | | | | GREGORY, R. | |
| | | | | SINCLAIR, A. | |
| | | | | GALT, B. | |
| | | | | RUSSELL, A. | |
| | | | | TAYLOR, G. | |
| | | | | MCCLEARY, W. (COX) | |
| 1924 | OLYMPICS | SILVER | FOURS W/O COX | BLACK, A.C. | VANCOUVER |
| | | | | WOOD, W. | |
| | | | | MACKAY, G.F. | |
| | | | | FINLAYSON, C.H.B. | |
| 1924 | OLYMPICS | SILVER | EIGHTS | CAMPBELL, I. | U. OF TORONTO R.C. |
| | | | | WALLACE, L. | |
| | | | | BELL, A. | |
| | | | | LANGFORD, W. | |
| | | | | HUNTER, R. | |
| | | | | SNYDER, W. | |
| | | | | SMITH, J. | |
| | | | | LITTLE, B. | |

| YEAR | EVENT | RESULT | RACE | CREW | CLUB |
|---|---|---|---|---|---|
| cont'd | OLYMPICS | SILVER | EIGHTS | TAYLOR, N. | |
| 1927 | HENLEY ROYAL | FINALIST | SINGLES | WRIGHT, JOE JR. | ARGONAUT R.C. |
| 1928 | HENLEY ROYAL | WIN | SINGLES | WRIGHT, JOE JR. | ARGONAUT R.C. |
| 1928 | OLYMPICS | SILVER | DOUBLES | WRIGHT, JOE JR. | ARGONAUT/DON R.C. |
| | | | | GUEST, JACK JR. | |
| 1928 | OLYMPICS | BRONZE | EIGHTS | ROSS, W.M. | ARGONAUT R.C. |
| | | | | NORRIS, C.E. | |
| | | | | MEECH, A.C. | |
| | | | | MURDOCK, J.L. | |
| | | | | RICHARDSON, H.T. | |
| | | | | HAND, J.L. | |
| | | | | FIDDES, F.J. | |
| | | | | HEDGES, F.C. | |
| | | | | DONNELLY, J.H. (COX) | |
| 1929 | HENLEY ROYAL | FINALIST | SINGLES | WRIGHT, JOE JR. | ARGONAUT R.C. |
| 1930 | HENLEY ROYAL | WIN | SINGLES | GUEST, JACK JR. | DON R.C. |
| 1930 | B.E.G. | GOLD | DOUBLES | BOLE, E. | WINNIPEG R.C. |
| | | | | RICHARDS, R. | |
| 1930 | B.E.G. | SILVER | FOURS W/O COX | MCCRAIG, H. | MCGILL UNIV. |
| | | | | GALES, L. | |
| | | | | EVANS, R. | |
| | | | | BUTLER, J. | |
| | | | | MILLS, A. (COX) | |
| 1930 | B.E.G. | SILVER | FOURS W/O COX | GAYNER, J. | JUBILEE B.C. HALIFAX |
| | | | | FLEMMING, J. | |
| | | | | BELLEW, O.G. | |
| | | | | PELHAM, H. | |
| 1930 | B.E.G. | BRONZE | EIGHTS | MOORE, W. | LEANDER, B.C. HAMILTON |
| | | | | BAWKS, L. | |
| | | | | FRY, H. | |
| | | | | ZABINSKY, J. | |
| | | | | THOBURN, W. | |
| | | | | BOAL, D. | |
| | | | | TAYLOR, A. | |
| | | | | EASTWOOD, E. | |
| | | | | MCDONALD, L. (COX) | |
| 1931 | HENLEY ROYAL | WIN | SINGLES | PEARCE, R. | LEANDER B.C. HAMILTON |
| 1932 | OLYMPICS | BRONZE | EIGHTS | EASTWOOD, E. | LEANDER B.C. HAMILTON |
| | | | | HARRIS, J. | |
| | | | | STANYAR, S. | |
| | | | | FRY, N. | |
| | | | | LIDDELL, C. | |
| | | | | THOBURN, W. | |
| | | | | BOAL, D. | |
| | | | | TAYLOR, A. | |
| | | | | MCDONALD, L. (COX) | |
| 1932 | OLYMPICS | BRONZE | DOUBLES | PRATTE, C.E. | VANCOUVER R.C. |
| | | | | DE MILLE, NOEL | |
| 1938 | B.E.G. | BRONZE | FOURS W/ COX | MCDONALD, J. | JAMES BAY A.A. |
| | | | | DAVIS, D. | |
| | | | | TEMPLE, J. | |
| | | | | WINKLER, M. | |
| | | | | JAGGARD, K. (COX) | |
| 1939 | HENLEY ROYAL | FINALIST | EIGHTS | RUDD, C.W. | ARGONAUT R.C. |
| | | | | CAMPBELL, C.A. | |

| YEAR EVENT | RESULT | RACE | CREW | CLUB |
|---|---|---|---|---|
| *cont'd* HENLEY ROYAL | FINALIST | EIGHTS | RUSSELL, J. / MINGAY, J. / COULSON, J.F. / DUNCAN, G. / SCOTT, R. / GAUDEUR, K. / DONNELLY, J. (COX) | |
| 1954 B.E.G. | GOLD | EIGHTS | SMITH, G.W. / HARRIS, T.M. / TOYNBEE, T.A. / MCDONALD, D.J. / WEST, L.K. / KOVITS, J.H. / DRUMMOND, K.J. / WILSON, R.A. / SIERPINA, R.J. (COX) | VANCOUVER R.C. |
| 1954 B.E.G. | BRONZE | DOUBLES | GUEST, D. / STEPHAN, L.D. | ARGONAUT R.C. |
| 1954 B.E.G. | BRONZE | SINGLES | WILLIAMS, ROBT. | LEANDER B.C. |
| 1955 HENLEY ROYAL | FINALIST | EIGHTS | SMITH, G.W. / HARRIS, T.M. / WEST, L.K. / MCDONALD, D.J. / TOYNBEE, T.A. / KOVITS, J.H. / HUGHES, W. / KUEBER, P.T. / OGAWA, C.S. (COX) | VANCOUVER R.C. |
| 1956 OLYMPICS | GOLD | FOURS W/O COX | ARNOLD, D.J. / D'HONDT, I.W. / LOOMER, L.K. / MACKINNON, A.A. | VANCOUVER R.C. |
| 1956 OLYMPICS | SILVER | EIGHTS | WEST, L.K. / MCDONALD, D.J. / MCKERLICH, W.A. / PRETTY, D.W. / HELLIWELL, D.L. / WILSON, R.A. / MCCLURE, R.N. / KUEBER, P.T. / OGAWA, C.S. (COX) | VANCOUVER R.C. |
| 1956 HENLEY ROYAL | FINALIST | FOURS W/O COX | ROONEY, J.F. / MCBRATNEY, A.C. / CODY, M.P. / ROONEY, V.J. | BROCKVILLE R.C. |
| 1958 B.E.G. | GOLD | EIGHTS | LOOMER, L.K. / PRETTY, D.W. / MERVYN, G.A. / D'HONDT, I.W. / MCKERLICH, W.A.M. / MACKINNON, A.A. / ARNOLD, D.J. / WILSON, R.A. / BILN, S. (COX) | VANCOUVER R.C. |
| 1958 B.E.G. | SILVER | FOURS W/O COX | SMITH, G.W. / TURNBULL, M.A. | VANCOUVER R.C. |

| YEAR EVENT | RESULT | RACE | CREW | CLUB |
|---|---|---|---|---|
| *cont'd* B.E.G. | SILVER | FOURS W/O COX | MCCLURE, R.N. / MADDEN, J.C.W. | |
| 1958 B.E.G. | SILVER | FOURS W/COX | ARNOLD, D.J. / HELLIWELL, D.L. / STAPLETON, W.L. / D'HONDT, I.W. / BILN, S. (COX) | VANCOUVER R.C. |
| 1959 PANAMS | SILVER | EIGHTS | ROBBINS, P. / D'HONDT, I.W. / MERVYN, G.A. / TURNBULL, M.A. / ANDERSON, D.A.H. / MADDEN, J.C.W. / BEARDMORE, I.M. / CARTMEL, J.L. / BILN, S. (COX) | VANCOUVER R.C. |
| 1959 PANAMS | SILVER | SINGLES | BIERNACKI, A. | OTTAWA R.C. |
| 1960 OLYMPICS | SILVER | EIGHTS | MERVYN, G.A. / D'HONDT, I.W. / MCKERLICH, W.A. / KUHN, N. / ARNOLD, D.J. / MACKINNON, A.A. / ANDERSON, D.A.H. / LECKY, J.H.S. / BILN, S. (COX) | VANCOUVER R.C. |
| 1962 COMMONWEALTH | BRONZE | FOURS W/O COX | WOROBIEFF, E. / GRAY, T.L. / STOKES, T.M. / MCINTOSH, R.A. | VANCOUVER R.C. |
| 1963 PANAMS | GOLD | EIGHTS | STURDY, D.R. / LEMIEUX, M. / WOROBIEFF, E. / GRAY, T.L. / MCINTOSH, R.A. / DEWAR, D.G. / BROWNE, T.P. / STOKES, T.M. / OVERTON, D. (COX) | VANCOUVER R.C. |
| 1964 OLYMPICS | GOLD | PAIRS W/O COX | JACKSON, R. / HUNGERFORD, G. | VANCOUVER R.C. |
| 1967 PANAMS | SILVER | EIGHTS | MCDANIEL, R.B. / MCAVITY, E.O. / RICHARDSON, J.O. / SJOGREN, C. / CHAPMAN, W.R. / CHAPMAN, F.J. / JOHNSON, B. / NOBLE, A.B. / CRAWLEY, H.F. (COX) | VANCOUVER R.C. |
| 1967 PANAMS | SILVER | FOURS W/O COX | CLARK, B.B. / WEBBER, P.B. / NETUPSKY, A.B. / FEARN, R.N. | VANCOUVER B.C. |
| 1967 PANAMS | SILVER | DOUBLES | CLARK, DOUG / GOTFREDSEN, L. | ARGONAUT R.C. |

| YEAR | EVENT | RESULT | RACE | CREW | CLUB |
|---|---|---|---|---|---|
| 1970 | HENLEY ROYAL | WIN | EIGHTS | WEINSTEIN, J. / SANYE, L. / VERITY, W. / SCHMON, R. / GIDNEY, D. / LONGSTAFF, S. / RUMBLE, L. / AZIZ, W. / HALLIDAY, B. (COX) | RIDLEY COLLEGE |
| 1971 | PANAMS | BRONZE | EIGHTS | SMITH, E.M. / JONKER, K.A. / BELL-IRVING, R. / NEARY, M.J. / ADVENT, R.S. / WALKER, J. / CUNLIFFE, R.M. / GORDON, I.M. / CONWAY, M.C. (COX) | VANCOUVER R.C. |
| 1972 | HENLEY ROYAL | WIN | FOURS W/ COX | CROOKER, R. / VANRUYVEN, A. / SYMSYCK, R. / QUAST, G. / HOOPLE, P. (COX) | ST. CATHARINES R.C. |
| 1973 | HENLEY ROYAL | WIN | EIGHTS | DORLAND, S. / COOPER, L. / CRASSWELLER, O. / POWELL, T. / BRAUL, H. / MCELHENNY, D. / MACLACHLAN, R. / MACKAY, R. / WALKER, R. (COX) | RIDLEY COLLEGE |
| 1973 | FISA YOUTH CHAMPIONSHIPS | BRONZE | MEN PAIR W/ COX | CARPENTER, B. / JOSTMAN, A. / NEWMAN, M. (COX) | ST. CATHARINES R.C |
| 1975 | PANAMS | GOLD | FOURS W/ COX | DICK, B. / BURAK, R. / MONKTON, P. / VANRUYVEN, A. / CHOQUETTE, B. (COX) | ST. CATHARINES R.C. |
| 1975 | PANAMS | SILVER | PAIR W/ COX | HENNIGER, J. / LOVE, B. / BATTERSBY, M. (COX) | VANCOUVER/ HANLAN R.C. |
| 1975 | PANAMS | BRONZE | FOURS W/O COX | GORDON, I.M. / MORROW, A. / NEARY, J.M. / MORAN, M.M. | VANCOUVER R.C. |
| 1975 | FISA YOUTH CHAMPIONSHIPS | BRONZE | MEN PAIR W/O COX | EVANS, M. / BRITTON-FOSTER, T. | HANLAN B.C. |
| 1975 | HENLEY ROYAL | WIN | EIGHTS | PORTER, C. / STEWART, W. / BERKHOUT, E. / REID, R. / BERKHOUT, L. / POS, M. / THETFORD, S. | RIDLEY COLLEGE |
| cont'd | HENLEY ROYAL | WIN | EIGHTS | MACLACHLAN, R. / WALKER, P. (COX) | |
| 1976 | HENLEY ROYAL | WIN | FOURS W/O COX | ALLESTER, J.T. / MORAN, M.M. / BODNAR, J.R. / RAE, K.A. | VANCOUVER R.C. |
| 1977 | WORLD CHAMPIONSHIPS | BRONZE | WOMEN EIGHTS | FERA, J. / NEULAND, C. / JACKLIN, K. / SMITH, T. / YOUNG, D. / HIGGINS, N. / DELURE, M. / EASTMURE, C. / SMITH, I. (COX) | BURNABY A.C./ ST. CATHARINES R.C. |
| 1977 | WORLD CHAMPIONSHIPS | BRONZE | WOMEN PAIR W/O COX | CRAIG, B. / ANTOFT, S. | BROCKVILLE/ HANLAN |
| 1977 | HENLEY ROYAL | WIN | EIGHTS | GREENWOOD, P. / DORLAND, P. / CHRISTIE, W. / JEFFERY, P. / VANDERBURGH, J. / HOPMANS, J. / MESSER, A. / CHAPLIN, R. / MCMAHON, B. (COX) | RIDLEY COLLEGE |
| 1978 | WORLD CHAMPIONSHIPS | SILVER | WOMEN PAIR W/O COX | CRAIG, B. / ANTOFT, S. | BROCKVILLE/ HANLAN |
| 1978 | WORLD CHAMPIONSHIPS | BRONZE | WOMEN EIGHTS | SMITH, T. / YOUNG, D. / GORDON, K. / JACKLIN, K. / DRAEGER, M. / CORT, G. / NEULAND, C. / FERA, J. / FLYNN, T. (COX) | BURNABY A.C./ ST. CATHARINES R.C./WOODSTOCK R.C. |
| 1978 | FISA YOUTH CHAMPIONSHIPS | BRONZE | WOMEN EIGHTS | TREGUNNO, J. / FAIR, M. / ROMAK, M. / CLARKE, C. / MACLAURIN, R. / CHAPMAN, K. / MAY, S. / CYBULSKI, C. / ANDERSON, L. (COX) | LONDON R.C./ WOODSTOCK R.C. |
| 1979 | PANAMS | GOLD | PAIR W/O COX | DICK, B. / STORM, T. | ST. CATHARINES R.C. |
| 1979 | PANAMS | GOLD | DOUBLE | FORD, B. / WALTER, P. | VIC. CITY R.C. |
| 1979 | PANAMS | SILVER | EIGHTS | RICHARDSON, J.O. / WITHERS, F.G. / FELIX, M. / HARTVIKSON, R.A. / WILKINSON, D.P. / CATHERALL, R. | VANCOUVER R.C. |

| YEAR | EVENT | RESULT | RACE | CREW | CLUB |
|---|---|---|---|---|---|
| cont'd | PANAMS | SILVER | EIGHTS | ORR, D. / HOOD, G. / CONWAY, M.C. (COX) | |
| 1979 | PANAMS | SILVER | FOUR W/ COX | CHERWINSKI, B. / TURTON, D. / LAFORME, M. / ZINTEL, C. / COHEN, M. (COX) | LEANDER B.C. |
| 1979 | PANAMS | SILVER | SINGLES | MONKTON, P. | RIDLEY GRADUATES |
| 1979 | FISA LIGHTWEIGHT CHAMPIONSHIPS | GOLD | SINGLES | THORNE,B. | ST .CATHARINES |
| 1979 | FISA YOUTH CHAMPIONSHIPS | GOLD | EIGHTS | VANHELVERT, S. / GRIEPSMA, E. / TREGUNNO, J. / ROMAK, M. / WETZL, S. / CYBULSKI, C. / SCHERTZING, Y. / ZUCCO, L. / DOBBING, H. (COX) | ST. CATHARINES R.C./CORNWALL R.C./SOUTH NIAGARA R.C./ WOODSTOCK R.C. |
| 1979 | HENLEY ROYAL | WIN | EIGHTS | WILSON, M. / HAAS, J. / POWELL, B. / LLOYD, C. / BRISTOW, T. / WODCHIS, M. / FITZPATRICK, D. / FERGUSON, C. / MCMAHON, B. (COX) | RIDLEY COLLEGE |
| 1980 | HENLEY ROYAL | WIN | DOUBLES | WALTER, P. / FORD, B. | VICTORIA CITY R.C. |
| 1980 | FISA YOUTH CHAMPIONSHIPS | BRONZE | WOMEN FOURS W/ COX | MILLEJOURS, K. / DAVIS, K. / VANDERLEE, J. / DAVIS, W. / WIKOBRADO, J. (COX) | SOUTH NIAGARA R.C./PETERBO-ROUGH/ST. CATHARINES |
| 1981 | HENLEY ROYAL | WIN | WOMEN DOUBLE | ROY, LISA / MASON, JANICE | VIC. CITY / VIC. CITY |
| 1981 | HENLEY ROYAL | WIN | MEN FOUR W/O COX | TURNER, TIM / TURNER, PAT / RELLE, JIM / GIBSON, TED | HANLAN / HANLAN / HANLAN / HANLAN |
| 1981 | WORLD CHAMPIONSHIPS | BRONZE | MEN FOUR W/O COX | RELLE, JAMES / TURNER, TIM / GIBSON, TED / TURNER, PAT | HANLAN / HANLAN / HANLAN / HANLAN |
| 1981 | WORLD CHAMPIONSHIPS | BRONZE | MEN LIGHTWEIGHT SINGLES | THORNE, BRIAN | ST. CATHARINES |
| 1981 | WORLD CHAMPIONSHIPS | SILVER | WOMEN PAIR W/O COX | SMITH, TRICIA / CRAIG, BETTY | VANCOUVER / BROCKVILLE |
| 1982 | UNIVERSIADE | GOLD | MEN SINGLE | HAMILTON, DOUG | KINGSTON |
| 1982 | WORLD CHAMPIONSHIPS | BRONZE | WOMEN DOUBLE | ROY, LISA / MASON, JANICE | VIC. CITY / VIC. CITY |
| 1982 | WORLD CHAMPIONSHIPS | BRONZE | WOMEN PAIR W/O COX | CRAIG, BETTY / SMITH, TRICIA | BROCKVILLE / VANCOUVER |
| 1983 | PANAMS | SILVER | MEN SINGLE | LAFORME, MEL | LEANDER |
| 1983 | PANAMS | BRONZE | MEN FOUR W/ COX | TOULMIN, NICK / STEELE, PAUL / JOHNSON, DAVID / BURAK, RON / TESSIER, PAUL (COX) | VIC. CITY / VRC / ARGONAUT R.C. / ST. CATHARINES / VIC. CITY |
| 1983 | PANAMS | SILVER | WOMEN DOUBLE | HATTIN, HEATHER / GAUDET, MARIE-CLAUDE | DON / BOUCHERVILLE |
| 1983 | PANAMS | BRONZE | WOMEN SINGLE | GRACE, MAUREEN | THUNDER BAY |
| 1983 | PANAMS | GOLD | MEN QUAD | MILLS, ROBERT / LAFORME, MEL / MURPHY, GREG JR. / HAGGERTY, PHIL | NORTH STAR / LEANDER / ST. CATHARINES / VIC. CITY |
| 1983 | PANAMS | BRONZE | MEN LIGHTWEIGHT FOUR W/O COX | LOUCKS, FRED / WILHELM, JOE / THOMAS, MARK / MAY, GARY | ST. CATHARINES / ST. CATHARINES / ST. CATHARINES / ST. CATHARINES |
| 1983 | PANAMS | BRONZE | MEN EIGHT | TESSIER, PAUL (COX) / WILKINS, GRAHAM / BURAK, RON / HORN, BLAIR / STEELE, PAUL / BRISTOW, TIM / BACKER, HAROLD / TOULMIN, NICK | VIC. CITY / PETERBOROUGH / ST. CATHARINES / VIC. CITY / VRC / RIDLEY GRADUATES / VRC / VIC. CITY |
| 1983 | PANAMS | GOLD | MEN DOUBLE | HAGGERTY, PHIL / MILLS, ROBERT | VIC. CITY / NORTH STAR |
| 1983 | WORLD CHAMPIONSHIPS | BRONZE | WOMEN PAIR W/O COX | CRAIG, BETTY / SMITH, TRICIA | BROCKVILLE / VRC |
| 1984 | WORLD CHAMPIONSHIPS | BRONZE | WOMEN LIGHTWEIGHT DOUBLE | MOWCHENKO, AUDREY / GILLIES, ELLEN | REGINA / REGINA |
| 1984 | OLYMPICS | BRONZE | MEN SINGLE | MILLS, ROBERT | NORTH STAR |
| 1984 | OLYMPICS | BRONZE | MEN QUAD | HUGHES, MICHAEL / FORD, BRUCE / HAMILTON, DOUG / MONKTON, PHIL | ST CATHARINES / VIC. CITY / KINGSTON / WESTERN |
| 1984 | OLYMPICS | SILVER | WOMEN PAIR W/O COX | CRAIG, BETTY / SMITH, TRICIA | BROCKVILLE / VRC |
| 1984 | OLYMPICS | SILVER | WOMEN FOUR W COX | SCHNEIDER, ANGIE / BRAIN, MARILYN / ARMBRUST, BARBARA / TREGUNNO, JANE / THOMPSON, LESLEY (COX) | ST CATHARINES / U. VIC / ST. CATHARINES / ST.CATHARINES / WESTERN |
| 1984 | OLYMPICS | GOLD | EIGHT | HORN, BLAIR / EVANS, MIKE / MAIN, GRANT / STEELE, PAUL / CRAWFORD, DEAN / TURNER, PAT / EVANS, MARK / MCMAHON, BRIAN (COX) / NEUFELD, KEVIN | VRC / HANLAN / VRC / VRC / VRC / HANLAN / HANLAN / RIDLEY GRADUATES / U. VIC |
| 1984 | OLYMPICS | BRONZE | WOMEN DOUBLE | LAUMANN, SILKEN / LAUMANN, DANIELLE | DON / DON |
| 1985 | HENLEY ROYAL | WIN | EIGHTS | SILK, H.J.M. / MACKAY, G.A. / BERKHOUT, D.G. | RIDLEY COLLEGE |

| YEAR | EVENT | RESULT | RACE | CREW | CLUB |
|---|---|---|---|---|---|
| cont'd | HENLEY ROYAL | WIN | EIGHTS | KRAIK, S.J. | |
| | | | | COY, T.A. (COX) | |
| | | | | PICKEN, R.G. | |
| | | | | MCKEOUGH, J.G. | |
| | | | | BRYDEN, D.J. | |
| | | | | MACMILLAN, I. | |
| 1985 | WORLD CHAMPIONSHIPS | GOLD | QUAD | MILLS, ROBERT | NORTH STAR |
| | | | | LAFORME, MEL | LEANDER |
| | | | | HAMILTON, DOUG | KINGSTON |
| | | | | DOUMA, PAUL | ST. CATHARINES |
| 1985 | WORLD CHAMPIONSHIPS | BRONZE | WOMEN FOUR W/ COX | ROBERTSON, LISA | U. VIC |
| | | | | SMITH, TRICIA | VRC |
| | | | | CLARKE, CHRISTINA | VRC |
| | | | | THOMPSON, LESLEY (COX) | WESTERN |
| | | | | ARMBRUST, BARBARA | ST. CATHARINES |
| 1986 | HENLEY ROYAL | WIN | EIGHTS | MACFARLANE, W.D. | RIDLEY COLLEGE |
| | | | | MACKAY, G.A. | |
| | | | | MCKEOUGH, J.G. | |
| | | | | BOYLE, D.S. | |
| | | | | COY, T.A. (COX) | |
| | | | | EVANS, H.D. | |
| | | | | PICKEN, R.G. | |
| | | | | WALKER, W.G. | |
| | | | | SILK, H.J.M. | |
| 1986 | COMMONWEALTH GAMES | SILVER | WOMEN SINGLE | WRIGHT, LISA | ST. CATHARINES |
| 1986 | COMMONWEALTH GAMES | SILVER | LIGHT SINGLE | TATTERSALL, PETER | KINGSTON |
| 1986 | COMMONWEALTH GAMES | BRONZE | WOMEN LIGHT SINGLE | HATTIN, HEATHER | DON |
| 1986 | COMMONWEALTH GAMES | GOLD | WOMEN PAIR | BARR, KATHRYN | ST. CATHARINES |
| | | | | SCHREINER, ANDREA | ST. CATHARINES |
| 1986 | COMMONWEALTH GAMES | BRONZE | LIGHT FOUR W/O COX | TIERNEY, RYAN | ST. CATHARINES |
| | | | | PEAKER, BRIAN | LONDON |
| | | | | THOMAS, ROBERT | LONDON |
| | | | | HENRY, DAVE | LONDON |
| 1986 | COMMONWEALTH GAMES | GOLD | FOUR W/O COX | STEELE, PAUL | VANCOUVER |
| | | | | NEUFELD, KEVIN | U. VIC |
| | | | | TURNER, PAT | HANLAN |
| | | | | MAIN, GRANT | VANCOUVER |
| 1986 | COMMONWEALTH GAMES | BRONZE | WOMEN LIGHT FOUR W/O COX | VANDERHORST, MARLENE | BURNABY LAKE AC |
| | | | | DROST, ANNE | ST. CATHARINES |
| | | | | WIEBE, WENDY | ST CATHARINES |
| | | | | HAMILTON, MARNIE | VIC. CITY |
| 1986 | COMMONWEALTH GAMES | GOLD | WOMEN FOUR W/ COX | DOEY/WALLINGA, JENNIFER | PETERBOROUGH |
| | | | | THOMPSON, LESLEY (COX) | WESTERN |
| | | | | CLARKE, CHRISTINA | VANCOUVER |
| | | | | SMITH, TRICIA | VANCOUVER |
| | | | | TREGUNNO, JANE | ST.CATHARINES |
| 1986 | COMMONWEALTH GAMES | BRONZE | WOMEN EIGHT | TREGUNNO, JANE | ST.CATHARINES |
| | | | | BARR, KATHRYN | ST. CATHARINES |
| | | | | CLARKE, CHRISTINA | VANCOUVER |
| | | | | CAMPBELL, MARILYN | KENNEBECASIS |
| | | | | DOEY/WALLINGA, JENNIFER | PETERBOROUGH |
| | | | | SMITH, TRICIA | VRC |
| | | | | SCHREINER, ANDREA | ST. CATHARINES |
| | | | | THOMPSON, LESLEY (COX) | WESTERN |
| | | | | ARMBRUST, BARBARA | ST. CATHARINES |
| 1986 | COMMONWEALTH GAMES | SILVER | WOMEN DOUBLE | CLARKE, HEATHER | WESTERN |

| YEAR | EVENT | RESULT | RACE | CREW | CLUB |
|---|---|---|---|---|---|
| cont'd | COMMONWEALTH GAMES | SILVER | WOMEN DOUBLE | ROBERTSON, LISA | U. VIC |
| 1986 | COMMONWEALTH GAMES | GOLD | DOUBLE | WALTER, PAT | BLAC |
| | | | | FORD, BRUCE | VIC. CITY |
| 1986 | FISA CHAMPIONSHIPS FOR JUNIORS | BRONZE | WOMEN PAIR W/O COX | JESPERSEN, JULIE | VIC. CITY |
| | | | | MCBEAN, MARNIE | WESTERN |
| 1986 | FISA CHAMPIONSHIPS FOR JUNIORS | BRONZE | FOUR W/O COX | BARBER, DARREN | BRENTWOOD |
| | | | | HABKIRK, CRAIG | BRENTWOOD |
| | | | | KENNEDY, IAN | SHAWNIGAN |
| | | | | HARPER, AL | CALGARY |
| 1986 | WORLD CHAMPIONSHIPS | BRONZE | QUAD | MILLS, ROBERT | NORTH STAR |
| | | | | LAFORME, MEL | LEANDER |
| | | | | DOUMA, PAUL | ST. CATHARINES |
| | | | | HAMILTON, DOUG | KINGSTON |
| 1986 | WORLD CHAMPIONSHIPS | BRONZE | WOMEN FOUR W/ COX | SMITH, TRICIA | VRC |
| | | | | THOMPSON, LESLEY (COX) | WESTERN |
| | | | | CLARKE, CHRISTINA | VRC |
| | | | | TREGUNNO, JANE | ST.CATHARINES |
| | | | | DOEY/WALLINGA, JENNIFER | PETERBOROUGH |
| 1986 | WORLD CHAMPIONSHIPS | BRONZE | LIGHT DOUBLE | HARVEY, CAM | DON |
| | | | | HAAG, ROBERT | DON |
| 1987 | FISA CHAMPIONSHIPS FOR JUNIORS | BRONZE | WOMEN PAIR | WALKER, SUE | RIDLEY GRADUATES |
| | | | | JESPERSEN, JULIE | U. VIC |
| 1987 | HENLEY ROYAL | FINALIST | EIGHTS | NEUFELD, KEVIN | U. VIC |
| | | | | WALLACE, JOHN | VIC. CITY |
| | | | | ROSS, DAVID | VANCOUVER |
| | | | | TELFER, DON | CALGARY |
| | | | | MCMAHON, BRIAN (COX) | RIDLEY GRADUATES |
| | | | | MAIN, GRANT | VANCOUVER |
| | | | | STEELE, PAUL | VANCOUVER |
| | | | | TURNER, PAT | HANLAN |
| | | | | CROSBY, ANDY | LEANDER |
| 1987 | HENLEY ROYAL | WIN | QUAD | LAFORME, MEL | LEANDER |
| | | | | DOUMA, PAUL | ST. CATHARINES |
| | | | | HAMILTON, DOUG | KINGSTON |
| | | | | MILLS, ROBERT | NORTH STAR |
| 1987 | PANAMS | SILVER | PAIR W/O COX | BERKHOUT, DARBY | RIDLEY GRADUATES |
| | | | | SCHAFFER, JAMES | VIC. CITY |
| 1987 | PANAMS | BRONZE | WOMEN DOUBLE | DELISLE, CONNIE | U. VIC |
| | | | | ASHFORD, KAREN | ARGONAUT R.C. |
| 1987 | PANAMS | GOLD | LIGHTWEIGHT DOUBLE | MURPHY, JOHN | ST. CATHARINES |
| | | | | THORNE, BRIAN | ST. CATHARINES |
| 1987 | PANAMS | SILVER | WOMEN LIGHTWEIGHT DOUBLE | VANDERHORST, MARLENE | BURNABY LAKE |
| | | | | HERRON, SIOBHAN | ST. CATHARINES |
| 1987 | PANAMS | BRONZE | EIGHT | ROBERTSON, BRUCE | CALGARY |
| | | | | RASCHER, MIKE | BLAC |
| | | | | COLLIER, RAYMOND | VANCOUVER |
| | | | | COOPER, TREVOR (COX) | VANCOUVER |
| | | | | DROSSOS, STEVE | VANCOUVER |
| | | | | BERKHOUT, DARBY | RIDLEY GRADUATES |
| | | | | MALCOLM, IAN | |
| | | | | MCKERLICH, IAN | VANCOUVER |
| | | | | SCHAFFER, JAMES | VIC. CITY |
| 1987 | PANAMS | BRONZE | LIGHTWEIGHT FOUR W/O COX | KENT, TOM | ST.CATHARINES |
| | | | | ANDERSON, SCOTT | ST.CATHARINES |
| | | | | DROSSOS, STEVE | VRC |
| | | | | MCFARLANE, WAYNE | KENNEBECASIS |

| YEAR | EVENT | RESULT | RACE | CREW | CLUB |
|---|---|---|---|---|---|
| 1987 | PANAMS | BRONZE | FOUR W/O COX | COLLIER, RAYMOND | VRC |
| | | | | RASCHER, MIKE | BLAC |
| | | | | ROBERTSON, BRUCE | CALGARY |
| | | | | FLOOD, CHRIS | ST.CATHARINES |
| 1987 | PANAMS | SILVER | LIGHTWEIGHT PAIR W/O COX | MCFARLANE, WAYNE | KENNEBECASIS |
| | | | | FLOOD, CHRIS | ST.CATHARINES |
| 1987 | PANAMS | GOLD | WOMEN PAIR W/O COX | BARNES, KIRSTEN | U. VIC |
| | | | | HEDDLE, KATHLEEN | BLAC |
| 1987 | PANAMS | SILVER | WOMEN LT PAIR W/O COX | SMYLE, KAREN | VRC |
| | | | | SINNEGE, DIANE | ST.CATHARINES |
| 1987 | PANAMS | GOLD | WOMEN SINGLE | LAUMANN, SILKEN | DON |
| 1987 | PANAMS | GOLD | WOMEN LIGHT SINGLE | MURPHY, MICHELLE | MONTREAL |
| 1987 | UNIVERSIADE | BRONZE | SINGLE | MURPHY, JOHN | ST. CATHARINES |
| 1987 | UNIVERSIADE | BRONZE | WOMEN SINGLE | LAUMANN, SILKEN | DON |
| 1987 | UNIVERSIADE | BRONZE | FOUR W/ COX | BACKER, HAROLD | VRC |
| | | | | SAUNDERSON, BRIAN | VANCOUVER |
| | | | | SCHAFFER, JAMES | VIC, CITY |
| | | | | MARLAND, ROBERT | PETERBOROUGH |
| | | | | PAUL, TERRY (COX) | PETERBOROUGH |
| 1987 | WORLD CHAMPIONSHIPS | SILVER | LIGHTWEIGHT SINGLE | WRIGHT, DAVE | ST. CATHARINES |
| 1987 | WORLD CHAMPIONSHIPS | BRONZE | QUAD | HAMILTON, DOUG | KINGSTON |
| | | | | DOUMA, PAUL | ST. CATHARINES |
| | | | | MILLS, ROBERT | NORTH STAR |
| | | | | LAFORME, MEL | LEANDER |
| 1987 | WORLD CHAMPIONSHIPS | GOLD | WOMEN LIGHTWEIGHT DOUBLE | HATTIN, HEATHER | DON |
| | | | | MASON, JANICE | VIC. CITY |
| 1989 | UNIVERSIADE | SILVER | FOUR W/O COX | DOEY/WALLINGA, JENNIFER | PETERBOROUGH |
| | | | | BARNES, KIRSTEN | U. VIC |
| | | | | MCBEAN, MARNIE | WESTERN |
| | | | | HEDDLE, KATHLEEN | BLAC |
| 1989 | UNIVERSIADE | SILVER | LIGHTWEIGHT SINGLE | MURPHY, JOHN | ST. CATHARINES |
| 1989 | HENLEY ROYAL | FINALIST | EIGHTS | BRYDEN, M. | RIDLEY COLLEGE |
| | | | | PARTINGTON, R. | |
| | | | | MARTIN, A. | |
| | | | | CHANT, C. | |
| | | | | NAZAR, W. | |
| | | | | BAILLIE, P. | |
| | | | | YOUNGER, D. | |
| | | | | BRYDEN, P. | |
| | | | | DEMPSTER, L. (COX) | |
| 1990 | WORLD CHAMPIONSHIPS | BRONZE | WOMEN LIGHT DOUBLE | COLBY, BRENDA | DON |
| | | | | WIEBE, WENDY | ST. CATHARINES |
| 1990 | WORLD CHAMPIONSHIPS | SILVER | EIGHT | PAUL, TERRY (COX) | PETERBOROUGH |
| | | | | PORTER, DEREK | U. VIC |
| | | | | ROBERTSON, BRUCE | CALGARY |
| | | | | RASCHER, MIKE | BLAC |
| | | | | SAUNDERSON, BRIAN | WESTERN |
| | | | | MARLAND, ROBERT | DON |
| | | | | CROSBY, ANDY | LEANDER |
| | | | | BARBER, DARREN | U. VIC |
| | | | | WALLACE, JOHN | VIC. CITY |
| 1990 | WORLD CHAMPIONSHIPS | GOLD | WOMEN LIGHTWEIGHT FOUR W/O COX | BLOIS, JILL | FREDERICTON |
| | | | | MILLER, COLLEEN | WINNIPEG |
| | | | | STARR, RACHEL | ST. CATHARINES |
| | | | | SINNEGE, DIANE | ST. CATHARINES |
| 1990 | WORLD CHAMPIONSHIPS | SILVER | WOMEN SINGLE | LAUMANN, SILKEN | DON |
| 1991 | PANAMS | BRONZE | DOUBLE | DICKISON, DAVE | FREDERICTON |
| | | | | DICKISON, DON | FREDERICTON |
| 1991 | PANAMS | GOLD | WOMEN LIGHTWEIGHT PAIR W/O COX | DOOBENAN, NORI | WESTERN |
| | | | | FEATHERSTONE, LAURIE | ARGONAUT R.C. |
| 1991 | PANAMS | BRONZE | EIGHT | FRISCH, STEVE | VIC. CITY |
| | | | | KOSKI, MIKE | U. VIC. |
| | | | | FOREGERON, MIKE | VIC. CITY |
| | | | | SIEBERT, JOHN | CALGARY |
| | | | | MIEGE, D. (COX) | U. VIC. |
| | | | | BROWN, DAVID | ARGONAUT R.C. |
| | | | | SWAN, IAN | U. VIC. |
| | | | | LAMONT, ANDREW | CALGARY |
| | | | | BOULTER, BRUCE | U. VIC |
| 1991 | PANAMS | BRONZE | FOUR W/ COX | SWAN, IAN | U. VIC. |
| | | | | MIEGE, D. (COX) | U. VIC. |
| | | | | LAMONT, ANDREW | CALGARY |
| | | | | BOULTER, BRUCE | U. VIC. |
| | | | | BROWN, DAVID | ARGONAUT R.C. |
| 1991 | PANAMS | BRONZE | FOUR W/O COX | SPOONER, CHRIS | U. VIC. |
| | | | | STEVENSON, GREG | MONTREAL |
| | | | | KOSKI, MIKE | U. VICTORIA |
| | | | | SIEBERT, JOHN | CALGARY |
| 1991 | PANAMS | GOLD | WOMEN FOUR W/O COX | CRAWFORD, SHANNON | ARGONAUT R.C. |
| | | | | JESPERSEN, JULIE | U. VICTORIA |
| | | | | SEPP, DANA | WESTERN |
| | | | | WALSH, ANDREA | U. VIC. |
| 1991 | PANAMS | SILVER | PAIR W/O COX | FRISCH, STEVE | VIC. CITY |
| | | | | FOREGERON, MIKE | VIC. CITY |
| 1991 | PANAMS | SILVER | WOMEN PAIR W/O COX | CRAWFORD, SHANNON | ARGONAUT R.C. |
| | | | | JESPERSEN, JULIE | U. VIC |
| 1991 | PANAMS | SILVER | SINGLE | HALLETT, TODD | MIC MAC |
| 1991 | WORLD CHAMPIONSHIPS | GOLD | WOMEN EIGHT | BARNES, KIRSTEN | U. VIC |
| | | | | MONROE, JESSICA | VRC |
| | | | | HEDDLE, KATHLEEN | BLAC |
| | | | | DOEY/WALLINGA, JENNIFER | WESTERN |
| | | | | MAHON, KELLY | VIC. CITY |
| | | | | THOMPSON, LESLEY (COX) | LONDON |
| | | | | MCBEAN, MARNIE | WESTERN |
| | | | | TAYLOR, BRENDA | VIC. CITY |
| | | | | DELEHANTY, MEGAN | BLAC |
| 1991 | WORLD CHAMPIONSHIPS | SILVER | EIGHT | ROBERTSON, BRUCE | CALGARY |
| | | | | MARLAND, ROBERT | DON |
| | | | | SAUNDERSON, BRIAN | WESTERN |
| | | | | TELFER, DON | CALGARY |
| | | | | BARBER, DARREN | U. VIC |
| | | | | WALLACE, JOHN | VIC. CITY |
| | | | | PAUL, TERRY (COX) | PETERBOROUGH |
| | | | | PORTER, DEREK | U. VIC. |
| | | | | CROSBY, ANDY | LEANDER |
| | | | | RASCHER, MIKE | BLAC |
| 1991 | WORLD CHAMPIONSHIPS | GOLD | WOMEN FOUR W/O COX | MONROE, JESSICA | VRC |
| | | | | DOEY/WALLINGA, JENNIFER | WESTERN |
| | | | | BARNES, KIRSTEN | U. VIC |
| | | | | TAYLOR, BRENDA | VIC. CITY |
| 1991 | WORLD CHAMPIONSHIPS | GOLD | WOMEN PAIR W/O COX | MCBEAN, MARNIE | WESTERN |
| | | | | HEDDLE, KATHLEEN | BLAC |

| YEAR | EVENT | RESULT | RACE | CREW | CLUB |
|------|-------|--------|------|------|------|
| 1991 | WORLD CHAMPIONSHIPS | GOLD | SINGLE | LAUMANN, SILKEN | DON |
| 1991 | WORLD CUP | GOLD | SINGLE | LAUMANN, SILKEN | DON |
| 1992 | HENLEY ROYAL | WIN | DOUBLE | HALLETT, TODD | MICMAC |
| | | | | DICKISON, DON | FREDERICTON |
| 1992 | OLYMPICS | GOLD | EIGHT | FOREGERON, MIKE | VIC. CITY |
| | | | | MARLAND, ROBERT | DON |
| | | | | ROBERSTON, BRUCE | CALGARY |
| | | | | PORTER, DEREK | U. VIC |
| | | | | RASCHER, MIKE | BLAC |
| | | | | PAUL, TERRY (COX) | PETERBOROUGH |
| | | | | WALLACE, JOHN | VIC. CITY |
| | | | | CROSBY, ANDY | LEANDER |
| | | | | BARBER, DARREN | U. VIC |
| 1992 | OLYMPICS | GOLD | WOMEN EIGHT | MCBEAN, MARNIE | WESTERN |
| | | | | WORTHINGTON, KAY | DON |
| | | | | BARNES, KIRSTEN | U. VIC |
| | | | | THOMPSON, LESLEY (COX) | LONDON |
| | | | | DELEHANTY, MEGAN | BLAC |
| | | | | HEDDLE, KATHLEEN | BLAC |
| | | | | MONROE, JESSICA | VRC |
| | | | | CRAWFORD, SHANNON | ARGONAUT R.C. |
| | | | | TAYLOR, BRENDA | VIC. CITY |
| 1992 | OLYMPICS | GOLD | WOMEN FOUR W/O COX | WORTHINGTON, KAY | DON |
| | | | | MONROE, JESSICA | VRC |
| | | | | TAYLOR, BRENDA | VIC. CITY |
| | | | | BARNES, KIRSTEN | U. VIC |
| 1992 | OLYMPICS | GOLD | WOMEN PAIR W/O COX | HEDDLE, KATHLEEN | BLAC |
| | | | | MCBEAN, MARNIE | WESTERN |
| 1992 | OLYMPICS | BRONZE | SINGLE | LAUMANN, SILKEN | DON |
| 1992 | WORLD CHAMPIONSHIPS | SILVER | WOMEN LIGHTWEIGHT DOUBLE | DARVILL, MICHELLE | DON |
| | | | | MILLER, COLLEEN | WINNIPEG |
| 1992 | WORLD CHAMPIONSHIPS | BRONZE | WOMEN LIGHTWEIGHT FOUR W/O COX | BLOIS, JILL | FREDERICTON |
| | | | | FEATHERSTONE, LAURIE | ARGONAUT R.C. |
| | | | | TROC, RENATA | WESTERN |
| | | | | DOOBENEN, NORI | ARGONAUT R.C. |
| 1992 | WORLD CHAMPIONSHIPS | BRONZE | WOMEN LIGHTWEIGHT SINGLE | WIEBE, WENDY | ST. CATHARINES |
| 1993 | UNIVERSIADE | GOLD | WOMEN LIGHTWEIGHT SINGLE | WIEBE, WENDY | ST. CATHARINES |
| 1993 | UNIVERSIADE | GOLD | WOMEN LIGHTWEIGHT DOUBLE | STARR, RACHEL | WESTERN |
| | | | | DUNCAN, TRACY | SASKATOON |
| 1993 | UNIVERSIADE | GOLD | WOMEN EIGHT | MAHON, KELLY | VIC. CITY |
| | | | | WILKINSON, CLARE | DON |
| | | | | BOYCHUK, DAYNA | WESTERN |
| | | | | LUKE, THERESA | |
| | | | | ROBINSON, EMMA | |
| | | | | MAUNDER, MARIA | WESTERN |
| | | | | MEISNER, KIRSTEN | U. VIC. |
| | | | | TAVES, LANA | U. VIC. |
| | | | | CALDER, KIM (COX) | U. VIC. |
| 1993 | UNIVERSIADE | GOLD | PAIR W/O COX | GRAHAM, PHIL | PETERBOROUGH |
| | | | | BARBER, DARREN | U. VIC. |
| 1993 | UNIVERSIADE | GOLD | WOMEN QUAD | MCBEAN, MARNIE | WESTERN |
| | | | | MAHON, KELLY | VIC. CITY |
| | | | | DARVILLE, MICHEL | DON |
| | | | | O'GRADY, DIANE | WESTERN |
| 1993 | UNIVERSIADE | SILVER | WOMEN FOUR W/O COX | BOYCHUK, DAYNA | WESTERN |
| | | | | ROBINSON, EMMA | |
| | | | | MAUNDER, MARIA | WESTERN |
| | | | | TAVES, LANA | U. VIC. |
| 1993 | UNIVERSIADE | SILVER | WOMEN SINGLE | MCBEAN, MARNIE | WESTERN |
| 1993 | UNIVERSIADE | SILVER | SINGLE | PORTER, DEREK | PETERBOROUGH |
| 1993 | UNIVERSIADE | SILVER | WOMEN LIGHTWEIGHT PAIR W/O COX | FEATHERSTONE, L | ARGONAUT R.C. |
| | | | | BRINDAMOUR, M | VANCOUVER |
| 1993 | UNIVERSIADE | SILVER | QUAD | PORTER, DEREK | PETERBOROUGH |
| | | | | BARBER, DARREN | U. VIC. |
| | | | | GRAHAM, PHIL | PETERBOROUGH |
| | | | | FORGERON, MIKE | VIC. CITY |
| 1993 | UNIVERSIADE | BRONZE | EIGHT | WALSH, SHAWN | U. VIC. |
| | | | | WALKEY, JACK | VANCOUVER |
| | | | | SCHELLINK, MIKE | U. VIC. |
| | | | | RUTH, DUNCAN | U. VIC. |
| | | | | PLATT, MARK | |
| | | | | PARFITT, ADAM | VIC. CITY |
| | | | | CROMBIE, BRAD | MONTREAL |
| | | | | HUGHES, GORDON | U. VIC. |
| | | | | HEFFERNAN, SHAWN | PETERBOROUGH |
| | | | | BERTAGNOLLI, JAY (COX) | CALGARY |
| 1993 | UNIVERSIADE | BRONZE | LIGHTWEIGHT DOUBLE | HILTON, JEFF | VANCOUVER |
| | | | | BRAMBELL, JAMES | VIC. CITY |
| 1993 | UNIVERSIADE | BRONZE | LIGHTWEIGHT FOUR W/O COX | FONTAINE, ROB | VIC. CITY |
| | | | | STRBA, STEVE | LEANDER |
| | | | | DAVIDSON, CHRIS | ST. CATHARINES |
| | | | | HASSETT, GAVIN | U. VIC. |
| 1993 | WORLD CHAMPIONSHIPS | GOLD | SINGLE | PORTER, DEREK | PETERBOROUGH |
| 1993 | WORLD CHAMPIONSHIPS | GOLD | WOMEN LIGHTWEIGHT SINGLE | DARVILLE, MICHELLE | DON |
| 1993 | WORLD CHAMPIONSHIPS | SILVER | WOMEN SINGLE | MCBEAN, MARNIE | WESTERN |
| 1993 | WORLD CHAMPIONSHIPS | GOLD | WOMEN LIGHTWEIGHT DOUBLE | WIEBE, WENDY | ST. CATHARINES |
| | | | | MILLER, COLLEEN | WINNIPEG |
| 1993 | WORLD CHAMPIONSHIPS | BRONZE | WOMEN FOUR W/O COX | ROBINSON, EMMA | |
| | | | | CRAWFORD, SHANNON | ARGONAUT R.C. |
| | | | | JESPERSEN, JULIE | U. VIC. |
| | | | | MAHON, KELLY | VIC. CITY |
| 1993 | WORLD CHAMPIONSHIPS | GOLD | LIGHTWEIGHT EIGHT | COOKSON,CHRIS | ST. CATHARINES |
| | | | | FONTAINE, ROBERT | VIC. CITY |
| | | | | SOMERWIL, PETER | ST. CATHARINES |
| | | | | LAY, JAY | ST. CATHARINES |
| | | | | BOYES, DAVE | ST. CATHARINES |
| | | | | THOMPSON, B | U. VIC. |
| | | | | HASSET, GREG | U. VIC. |
| | | | | PEAKER, BRIAN | LONDON |
| | | | | NEWMAN, PAT (COX) | ST. CATHARINES |
| 1993 | WORLD CHAMPIONSHIPS | SILVER | LIGHTWEIGHT WOMEN FOUR W/O COX | HARRIMAN, MAUREEN | LEANDER |
| | | | | DOOBENEN, NORI | WESTERN |
| | | | | DUNCAN, TRACY | SASKATOON |
| | | | | STARR, RACHEL | WESTERN |

# ENDNOTES

1 Outriggers are metal cantilevers that attach to the side of the hull and allow the oarlock to be moved outside the hull and away from the oarsman, thus lengthening the leverage on the oar.

2 These boats were constructed of thick planks of wood, laid so as to overlap and provide both a measure of strength and a watertight hull.

3 Stroke sits as last man in the boat from the bow and is the pacesetter for the crew. Stroke is usually the athlete whose combination of style, stamina, physical fitness and strength is the best.

4 Under race conditions, the concentration of the crew should be complete. Interruptions, such as talking in the boat, are seen as distractions and will be resented, especially under the stress and strain of the last part of a race.

5 "Freedom of the city" is a term whose origins are to be found in medieval history. Freedom of the city gave permission to the recipient to behave in ways not permitted to all visitors and included the right to bear arms and not to pay taxes. Giving someone the keys to the city implied total surrender of the city, which is clearly more than giving the freedom.

6 The build of the boat was unique for the time. It was the first boat built as narrow as possible, to reduce resistance in the water. Compensation for the lack of width was achieved by increasing the length, but the boat was completely unstable and required great skill to row competently. The long, narrow design pioneered in this craft has remained to the present. The original is kept in Canada's Sport Hall of Fame in Toronto.

7 A word of warning, however: as in any outdoor sport, wind conditions will affect times over distances. In water sports, wind conditions also affect the water surface, and together the effects have a dramatic effect on the duration of a race. In rowing, therefore, no times are taken as absolute, and there is no longer an official world record for a rowing race.

8 The origins of the Royal prefix became a matter of debate in the 1980s when it was discovered that in fact no Royal Warrant had ever been issued. It appears that a member of the royal family visited the regatta 1908 and agreed to the royal patronage, but the steps were never taken. Her Majesty, Elizabeth II, agreed to the designation and the warrant is now official.

9 As late as 1950, clubs would hire a complete rail car and travel with their shells (including eights) to the regatta site. At some sites, rail sidings were close enough to the water that the car was used as a temporary home for boats and athletes. In some cases, clubs hired flat cars to carry the shells, but in others, the shells were taken into the passenger car itself. Entrance into the passenger rail car was by a door at the end, which opened straight onto the aisle down the centre of the car. Shells would be passed into the car through the end door and laid on the floor.

10 At the time of writing, Pierre Elliott Trudeau, who succeeded John Diefenbaker, is honourary president, and the mayor of Ottawa, Jacqueline Holzman, is honourary vice-president.

11 There is still some controversy over whether or not a regatta was held in 1916. Newspapers of the day carry a record of the event, but the trophy plaques do not record the winners. The Canadian Amateur Rowing Association nevertheless celebrated the hundredth Henley in 1991.

12 Canada was unique because it was the only country where women were welcomed to rowing in the existing (male) rowing association. In all other countries, women's rowing was conducted within an affiliated but separate association. Not until after 1976 did other national organizations follow Canada's lead.

# BIBLIOGRAPHY

Beedling, Paul. "'Young Joe': A Biography." Thesis, University of Western Ontario, 1980.

Boyd, Ian. "Not just any Ol' Joe: Joseph Wright Senior, Canada's Premier Rowing Coach." Student essay, University of Western Ontario, 1989.

Brooks, Stephanie. "An Athletic Biography of a Champion Sculler: Jacob Gill Gaudaur, 1858-1937." Master of Arts Thesis, University of Western Ontario, 1981.

Carver, John A. *The Vancouver Rowing Club*. Aubrey Roberts Ltd., 1980.

Clarke, Heather, and Susan Gwynne-Timothy. *Stroke*. James Lorimer and Co., 1988.

Corinne, Mol. "The History of Rowing in Victoria." Thesis, University of Victoria, 1984.

Cosentino, Frank. *Ned Hanlan*. The Canadians, a continuing series. Fitzhenry and Whiteside Limited, 1978.

Dodd, Christopher. *Boating*. Oxford University Press, 1983.

———. *The Story of World Rowing*. Stanley Paul, 1992.

Flood, Brian. *Saint John, A Sporting Tradition, 1785-1985*. Neptune Publishing Company Limited, 1985.

Graham, Frank W. *Ready...Set...Go! A St. John's Sports Pictorial*. Creative Publishers, 1988.

Hunter, Robert S. *Rowing in Canada Since 1848*. Davis Lisson Limited, 1933.

King, Peter. *Art and a Century of Canadian Rowing*. Amberley House Limited, 1980.

Warre, Edmund. *On the Grammar of Rowing*. Oxford University Press, 1909.